ENDORSEMENTS

Ed Sniadecki's *Warfare Realm* is a revelation masterpiece into personal spiritual warfare. We are on the precipice of an unprecedented move of God, and the old wineskins of ministry are beginning to pass away. God is accelerating the transformative process, and what used to take hours in ministry is now accomplished in minutes through the power of the Holy Spirit. Broken hearts are healed; demonic strongholds removed. Freedom is the result.

Warfare Realm parts the veil, giving us a glimpse of how the seven-fold Spirit of God works in ministry situations. It emphasizes the importance of teamwork, spiritual covering, and moving with the wisdom and unction of God. In essence, it is a revelatory picture of how we on MorningStar's Freedom Teams operate.

Through his prophetic visions, Ed brings insight into the healing heart of a loving heavenly Father. His book becomes an open door into our own encounters with God. It both inspires and beckons us to engage in the spiritual realm for healing and wholeness, first for ourselves and then for others. God is once again shining His holy light on this realm of ministry, and Ed's book reflects that glorious truth.

Pamela Palagyi, M.Div.
Head of the Healing and Freedom Teams at MorningStar Ministries

Author of *The Word Became Flesh: Studies in the Gospel of John*,
Empowered: A Practical Guide to Personal Ministry, and *Established: Seeking God's Plan for Spiritual Growth*

As a keen gardener, I often see parallels with the spiritual realm. This spring we had exceptional rain, and my plants, shrubs, trees, and flowers grew with great vigor. But so did the weeds, briars, thorns, and thistles. The Lord is pouring out His rain for good, but evil is also growing at an alarming rate.

Guided by the Holy Spirit, Ed demonstrates great sensitivity in uprooting the evil "plants" in this *Final Quest*-like journey into the *Warfare Realm*. It is what we are all called into for the days ahead. May you be enlightened by this illuminating work.

Derek Tripp
MorningStar Ministries Connect Group and Restoration Team,
England

I have known Ed and his family for many years. He has been a true friend in many ways. His love for the Lord has always been a first priority in everything he does. His time with the Lord and his inspirational writing remind me of Psalm 32:8, "I will instruct you and teach you in the way you should go;

I will counsel you with my loving eye on you." (NIV)

As I read, I feel he has put me in the story, and I am living out some of the same circumstances. Anyone reading this book and others he has written will have a strong desire to be up early and meet with the Father.

Dennis Jahn
Personal friend, involved in prison ministry

FOREWORD BY CHRIS REED

Spirit Realm Battles ✦ Book One

WARFARE REALM

ED SNIADECKI

Spirit Realm Battles ✦ Book One

WARFARE REALM

Warfare Realm
Book one, *Spirit Realm Battles*
By Ed Sniadecki

Copyright © 2024. Fort Mill, SC. All rights reserved.
ISBN: 9798334149274

Cover and Layout design: Kandi Evans

To contact the author: **coffeetime.chronicles@gmail.com**

CONTENTS

FOREWORD

Ed Sniadecki is a true gift to the body of Christ. For years he sought the Lord in daily early-morning devotional times. He began to understand the value of waiting upon the Lord and blessing his spirit.

In 2021, during one of his intimate times with the Lord, he pondered a message about Christ that changed him forever. Ed then had a powerful encounter. And every day after that the encounters continued. The Lord was telling Him profound truths through experiences and stories.

Ed has chronicled these prophetic encounters, which I can testify are real. He has given me prophetic words from these encounters that have been accurate.

Even though Ed is an elder at our church and a very gifted man, he also represents the laity—those who can encounter the Lord and know Him better. We are living in unprecedented times, and with that comes an unprecedented amount of spiritual warfare. The experiences Ed shares provide a roadmap to navigate spiritual warfare and maintain victory through these difficult times.

In the second heaven, there is ongoing warfare. The devil lost access to the third heaven before time began, and the book of Revelation tells us he will be cast out of the second heaven. Revelation 12 discusses this fall of Satan. Many believers can sense disturbing forces in the atmosphere because third-heaven realities are coming to earth soon, and second-heaven forces are resisting.

The second heaven is where demons and angels engage in warfare over our prayers and the souls of men and women. Understanding spiritual warfare changes how you view people, situations in the church, and the world. The weapons of our warfare are not carnal but mighty through God to the pulling down of strongholds. (2 Cor. 10:4)

This book will tremendously bless you. Ed's encounters provide deep insights into the spirit world, showing how we should and should not react. This is a blessing to the body of Christ.

Ed is my friend. He does not claim to be part of the fivefold ministry but represents the Church, used by God to access the spiritual realm. His spiritual eyes have been opened, and this is available to you as well. Reading these pages and learning about these encounters will help open your eyes too.

We need insight more than ever; we need to know the plans of heaven and the plans of hell to respond accordingly. We are often tempted to react to physical issues and not realize that spiritual forces are affecting what's happening in the natural realm. When our spiritual eyes and senses are open, we can see beyond the veil and understand what's really happening around us. This book is truly a treasure and will help you grow as you learn to bless your spirit and wait upon the Lord.

Waiting upon the Lord involves concentrating all of your being and thoughts, silencing the brain chatter, and simply saying, "Here I am, Holy Spirit. Speak, Lord, for Your servant is listening."

I love this book and all of Ed's books. I highly recommend that you read it. But don't just read it—immerse yourself in these encounters and let your Christianity become more than just a Sunday morning commitment. Let it become a lifestyle, a daily encounter with a living Christ.

~**Chris Reed**
CEO and President, Morningstar Ministries

DEDICATION

To everyone who has fought a battle in the spirit, may this book encourage you that there are more on our side than on the enemy's.

For though we walk in the flesh, we do not war according to the flesh. For the weapons of our warfare are not carnal but mighty in God for pulling down strongholds. (2 Cor. 10:3-4)

Mighty because we fight an unseen-to-the-natural-eye spiritual enemy with unseen-to-the-natural-eye spiritual weapons. The seven Spirits, expressed through Holy Spirit, are seen in the spirit realms where the battle is truly fought.

Fight on mighty warriors of the most high God. You are making progress.

ACKNOWLEDGMENTS

"Thank You, Papa," are the only English words I have. I can't fully express the overwhelming thankfulness and gratitude that I feel. The Creator of the universe continues to take me into His presence. Wow, Wow, Wow.

Chris, your amazing foreword. Thanks for taking the time out of your busy schedule to read and comment on this book.

John and Deb, once again your timeless hours of editing and putting all this together for people to read. Thank You.

You who have endorsed this book, thanks for believing in me enough to do that.

The introduction to this book is from the woman I've lived with for 43 years, my wife and best friend Lisa. Your words of introduction are off the charts. Thanks for standing with me in these encounters of His presence these past few years. I love you.

INTRODUCTION

I met my future husband, Ed, in Manhattan, New York, in 1981 during a business conference. For me, it was love at first sight. We have now been married 43 years.

One of the most attractive attributes Ed displayed in our early years together and which continues to this day is commitment. His devotion and commitment to me as a wife, to our four adult children as a father, and to our Lord is a stunning reality.

My husband's spiritual walk has deepened over the years, and it humbles me as I stand by his side.

Four years ago, he hungered for even more. During one of his daily early-morning prayer times, he said, "I don't know if I know Jesus!" Then Holy Spirit invited my husband into an ascended relationship, carrying him into realms that were unknown to him and us.

Ed's pure heart and childlike demeanor have attracted the God of the universe. H (Holy Spirit) often reminds Ed during these visitations that he has eternity to learn certain things.

It's my joy to introduce you to a very personal journey that both Ed and I have been on. Yahweh is looking for friends to spend time with and share secrets with.

In *Warfare Realm*, be prepared to have your mind blown. It's not what you think....

~Lisa

WARFARE REALM

Opening my eyes this morning, I see in front of and below me a meandering river. All is quiet. No sound comes from the river below or the sky above. I'm standing on a high ridge above the river. It goes off to my right for what looks like miles. The water is a light, hazy blue, reflecting the blue sky above.

Next to me on my right is a steel chain, a guard rail at the edge of the ridge I'm standing on as I look down at the river. The chain goes in front of me and leads off to my left. Reaching out with my right hand to grab it, I hear in my spirit, "This chain leads to a bridge that swings across the river to the other side."

Letting go of the chain, I say, "Good morning, Holy Spirit. Thanks for being here with me today."

"My pleasure," He says. "But I'm not alone. I have a few friends with Me this morning."

"Friends?" I think. "Awesome. I get to meet friends of Holy Spirit." I reply, "That's great. How many friends are with You?"

"Turn and see," He replies.

Turning to my left where His voice is coming from, I see a vast open plain but no people. Wondering, I ask, "Where are Your friends?"

"In the spirit," He says.

I think, "Am I in the spirit with You?"

Before I can ask, He says, "Yes and no."

"Yes and no?" I think back.

He replies, "Yes, you are in the spirit, and, no, you're not. You're sitting in your library chair."

"Okay," I reply, "this is where I'm at physically, but I thought You or Papa took me into the spirit realm."

"We do," He replies. "So ask for your eyes to be opened and your ears to hear."

I think, "Yes, I woke up only seeing part of what You have for me, only seeing part of the whole picture with no sound. Please forgive me. My excitement at seeing the river caused me to move in without asking to see and hear."

He says, "No need for forgiveness at this point. Today is a learning day for you to go beyond where you have seen and heard. Moving past where you have been will require more focus and more of Us guiding you. The next realm is a warfare realm."

At His words, I hesitate in my being. I say "being" because I believe the hesitation is a mix of my natural mind, will, and emotions flooding my spirit. Holy Spirit patiently waits next to me. "Am I ready for a warfare realm experience?" I ask.

"That's up to you," He replies. We have been taking you and showing you Our glory, Our presence, Our goodness, and reassuring you that We will never leave you or forsake you. That I am as close as a breath away. That the presence of Papa is in and on you and moves through you. You have understanding of the revelation that Jesus lives in you and is seated at the right hand of the Father in the heavenly realms while He is in you. So, yes, We believe you are ready. But do you believe you are ready?"

At His words I have a flashback of a little blue-eyed girl asking me a similar question from an encounter in the spirit I had many months ago. I see her piercing blue eyes and realize that she was speaking the words of

Holy Spirit into my spirit. Now it's Holy Spirit Himself speaking these words that cause me to ask myself, "Do I believe?"

My spirit bursts out, "Yes, I believe."

Instantly, I pray. "I call my spirit man forward and bless it to receive and move with Holy Spirit into this next realm. I tell my natural mind, will, and emotions to line up with my spirit who is out front. I bless this alignment of spirit, soul, and body to be in proper alignment and follow Holy Spirit. Please give me eyes to see and ears to hear."

All of a sudden, the river below is magnified in my hearing. The sound of a screeching eagle causes my head to shift to the right, and I see a company of eagles flying high above the river below.

To my left and behind me I hear a multitude of feet moving on the ground. My expectation is high, in anticipation of seeing the army I will see, all clad in armor ready to move forward and cross the bridge to the other side. Turning to see this army, these friends of Holy Spirit, what I see shocks me. It's a rag-tag bunch of unkempt people with no armor, some with no shoes--a mix of men, women, and children all huddled together in a small clump.

I lean into Holy Spirit and feel His excitement about what I'm seeing and ask, "Am I seeing correctly?" I feel more excitement oozing from Him into my spirit as He nods in the affirmative.

Then He says, "Yup, with one exception. You're looking at the out-side. Their armor is within, spirits tried in the fire and a determination to please the Father in all they do. These are common, everyday people just like you with whom We are working. People who see and hear what We have for them to see and hear. They, like you, are ready to go wherever We are taking them."

Then He points to another larger group of people gathered way out farther on the plain. I look to where He is pointing and see a group of well-dressed people, and even see a few swords.

He says, "Not ready. They are still moving past doubt and unbelief.

Those in front of you are some of Our finest, and they are ready to cross over with you."

I feel a slight breeze.

He says, "Yes, that's Me blowing off any remaining residue of a shadow of doubt from you and them. The river below will carry the dust of doubt far away."

I say with resolve, "Okay then, let's get moving."

He says, "One more thing. You all have battles to fight, and you all have a battle to fight. Your weapons, although not carnal, are on the other side. You know We are with you."

I nod my head and say, "Yes, Lord."

A sparkle catches my eye. I glance at what I called a rag-tag bunch to see a glimmer in their eyes that I didn't catch before. They have been waiting and anticipating crossing over into this warfare realm.

Holy Spirit whispers, "Now you are seeing rightly."

I look at this group of people, point to the bridge, and say, "Let's go." There's no hesitation, and I sense no doubt or fear. They are a group on a mission, and I'm here with them. I turn to the bridge, take a step forward, and "I'm moved back into the natural, sitting in my library chair. I breathe deeply and think, "This is a big one. They are taking me, us, into a realm Holy Spirit calls a warfare realm."

I pray out. "I, we, need Your help in this, Papa. I know You are and will be there. Amen."

STEP BY STEP

Standing in front of the vanity, looking into the mirror and shaving, I glance at my feet. With the razor in my right hand, shaving cream still on half my shaven face, I see through the vanity that my toes are hanging over the edge of a cliff.

I quickly grab for the vanity with my left hand, and I'm steadied. Whoa, I wasn't expecting that.

Slowly releasing the vanity, I see that I'm standing on a ridge, looking down into a vast valley with a river below. The razor in my right hand is replaced by the steel chain I grabbed the other day that leads to the bridge going to the warfare realm.

Then I'm back, the mirror in front of me. Steadying my hand, I finish shaving. Before getting to my library chair, I see, several more times, my feet on the edge of the cliff.

Now sitting in my library chair, I jokingly think, "Might be good to have a seat belt."

Holy Spirit whispers, "You got Me. No seat belt needed."

I say, "Thanks. Was that the bridge to the other side?"

He says, "Yes."

I ask, "Where is the bridge?" As I'm asking, I answer my own question and say the same words He is saying to me, "In the spirit."

Back on the ridge looking down at my feet, I notice a golden glow coming from under them. I also notice a little toe wiggle under my right little toe. What? I'm standing on another foot.

Holy Spirit is quick to say, "Feet of the Lord are under your feet. He is carrying you in this walk to the other side."

I respond, "This is a new perspective of being in Christ and Him being in me."

All Holy Spirit says is, "In, on, and around you all the time."

I reach out into nothing to grab the chain with my right hand. As I do, it appears. Looking ahead, I only see the chain going out in midair over the valley, and it disappears into a cloud about 50 feet away. I know the bridge is in the spirit, and I see the feet of the Lord carrying me, but I don't see a bridge or a chain on the left. This has to be a spirit-led walk, I cannot do this in the natural. I reassure myself that my spirit man is out front to continue this walk. I hear a sound on my left and see a hand reaching out past me on the left.

Holy Spirit whispers, "One of my friends, a rag-tag group member, as you called them."

I feel a body close to me and watch as the person's left hand reaches out into nothing and grabs a chain on the left side. I realize this is a team effort. Holy Spirit told me we were going over together. Looking down at my feet, I see the feet of the person next to me. His have a golden glow under them also.

Holy Spirit says, "Yes, this is a together team effort to get to the other side. You with them, and Jesus carrying all of you."

I hear the footsteps of the group behind us ready to go. Looking out at the two chains disappearing into the cloud in front of me, I still do not see a bridge. I think of the many times the Lord has given me only one word or shown me one picture to get started. Once I get started with what He has spoken to me or shown me, another word or picture comes. Before long the individual words or pictures complete the whole of what He has been giving me step by step. These are the words I needed, step by step, to encourage myself to take the first step, which in reality is Him lifting my feet and all our feet to take us to the other side.

My hand grips the chain tightly, so tightly I might not be able to let go to move along the chain. Then it occurs to me, "He's got this. Holy Spirit and His friends are here with me. The feet of the Lord are under my feet, and He has provided a way to cross over." I loosen my grip a bit on the chain. My right foot rises, and I lean into the nothing in front of me while looking down to see the foot of the man next to me in the air also. In unison we drop our feet to hit a solid surface of a bridge under our feet. I hear praises from the people behind. The left foot of the man next to me and my foot rise in unison and then are planted on another section of the bridge appearing under our feet.

Holy Spirit interjects, "Most times, all that people need is for someone to step out first, and they will follow."

I hear feet being placed on the bridge behind us. One by one we continue to take steps and move forward on the ever-appearing bridge under our feet as we walk in obedience to Him.

Holy Spirit interjects again, "You and the group with you are not just following a bridge across to the other side. Your obedience is creating a bridge to the other side for others to follow and cross over."

I think, "This is another big learning lesson."

Holy Spirit is quick to answer my thought, "Yes, it is, in more ways than you realize right now."

I wonder, "What does He mean by that?"

His thought back to me, "All in due time. All in due time. For now, you need to continue to focus on where you're heading. You are helping the group following you get to the other side by stepping where the Lord is showing you. For now, this is your mission, and this is your focus."

I respond, "Yes, Sir."

Before long we are in the cloud where the chains on the right and left disappeared. We are now walking along in a thick cloud--one foot up, one foot down, other foot up, other foot down. There is a presence, almost a light in this cloud, that I have not felt before. I ask, "Is this His covering presence?"

Holy Spirit says, "Yes, you're catching on. You have walked through this before, but you are noticing it now for what it is. His covering presence is here to shield you and them as you enter the warfare realm."

"This is good," I think back to Holy Spirit.

He responds, "Good is an understatement. This is really good that you're entering under the shadow of the Almighty."

I recall the verses in Exodus 14 when the Israelites were getting ready to enter the Red Sea, and the angel of the Lord moved the cloud. I paraphrase it in my mind, "To one it was light, and to the other it was darkness."

"Yes, this is a good way to look at it," Holy Spirit says.

Next question, "Are we close?" At the thought, I smile. I'm reminded of our young children in the car when we were going somewhere, asking, "Are we there yet?"

Holy Spirit says, "Human nature. We have been working with it since the garden. When We finally get you going, you get impatient to get there. The goal is the other side. You'll know when you're close and when you get there."

We continue to move along the bridge. A quick look back, and I see all are doing well, following close behind, no stragglers. I do notice I can't see the ridge where we disembarked.

I hear the whisper, "Focus."

I think, "Yes, Sir, just checking."

He says, "All is in check. Continue to focus."

I keep gazing directly in front of me but notice my feet are starting to feel heavy. I look down to see the golden glow is still there but diminishing under our feet.

I hear, "Your weapons are starting to become available. You need to pick them up."

I'm not seeing any weapons.

I hear back, "In the spirit."

I concentrate, "In the spirit. He is telling me, 'In the spirit.'" The verses, 2 Chronicles 20:20-21, come to mind.

So they rose early in the morning and went out into the Wilderness of Tekoa; and as they went out, Jehoshaphat stood and said, "Hear me, O Judah and you inhabitants of Jerusalem: Believe in the LORD your God, and you shall be established; believe His prophets, and you shall prosper." And when he had consulted with the people, he appointed those who should sing to the LORD, and who should praise the beauty of holiness, as they went out before the army and were saying:

"Praise the LORD,

For His mercy endures forever."

Then, in my spirit I hear words from a worship song, "My praise is a weapon."

"That's it!" I exclaim. We need to praise. Praise is our first weapon." I begin to praise, and the group follows suit. Soon we are all praising, and our steps again become lighter.

Holy Spirit speaks to our spirits, "Through the praises of Our people We are magnified. Through the praises of Our people We are glorified. Through the praises of Our people We release what's needed to supply the victory. Your praise is not only your weapon but also Our pathway through you.

"It won't be long now, and you will be on the other side. You must remember your first weapon is your most valuable weapon, your praise. Praise is like your sheath that encompasses all your weapons. There is only one greater than praise; it's the love of the Father Jesus spoke of in the Sermon on the Mount. Praise is the sheath, and the sheath is only strapped on by the Father's love. We will add more individual weapons as needed. Master these two to gain what will be needed when it's needed."

With this encouragement from Holy Spirit, we continue at a steady pace, knowing we are near. We have our sheaths of praise strapped on with the Father's love.

Another cloud appears in front of me. Entering it, I'm brought back to the natural to see my natural feet situated on the floor at the front of my chair.

"Wow," I think, "this trek on the bridge has once again brought revelation from Holy Spirit. There truly is a never-ending flow of what He has for us."

"I thank and praise you, Papa, for this new revelation. My praise is a weapon, not just words in a song! Amen! Amen!"

EVALUATION

The mind of my spirit replays the events leading up to the trek to the warfare realm. Holy Spirit was our constant Companion and Guide into this unknown realm. He took me into other realms, but I and the group with me need to walk into this one. Really, it was Jesus Who walked and carried us into this realm. He was even in the first step. We see, we feel, we move, and even get tired in the spirit. Our feet get heavy. But we were covered by the shadow of the Almighty.

All this is for us to benefit from what we learn in this unknown realm. Holy Spirit even said, "All in due time" twice when I commented about a learning lesson. He hinted there was more to come.

Also, He always referred to this realm as a "warfare realm," not a "realm of warfare." I know there's a lesson in that alone.

As I ponder, I'm brought back to the bridge with the group. It's like I never left.

We continue to walk along, one step in front of the other, the bridge appearing before us as we do. I look to my chest area and to the man next to me to see no sheath strapped onto either of us. The man, with his right hand, palm towards his chest, pats his chest a few times. Next, he reaches out and pats my chest. Finally, he points with his index finger into my heart. No words are spoken audibly. He is telling me spirit to spirit, the weapon is on the inside. This lines up with what Holy Spirit said when I met His friends. "Their armor is on the inside." It somehow makes sense. The scripture comes to mind from 2 Corinthians 10:3-6,

For though we walk in the flesh, we do not war according to the flesh. For the weapons of our warfare are not carnal but mighty in God for pulling down strongholds, casting down arguments and every high thing that exalts itself against the knowledge of God, bringing every thought into captivity to the obedience of Christ, and being ready to punish all disobedience when your obedience is fulfilled.

The love of the Father is the strap securing the sheath of praise to carry the weapons. If the weapons are in my hands, it means I will use them. If they are activated from the heart, the love of the Father, He is using them. I wonder if this is part of the more Holy Spirit was hinting at.

I look at my feet and the feet of the man next to me again. The golden glow still radiates from under them, but now the gold is not just under our feet. It's extended and strapped onto our feet. I'm beginning to understand what Ephesians 6:15 says, *"Having shod your feet with the preparation of the gospel of peace."*

This is the manifestation of the armor and weapons being applied to my spirit man. As I continue to walk along the bridge, I feel a difference in my walk. My step is lighter, and an illuminating glow shines from under my feet.

"Yes," I hear Holy Spirit say.

At His "yes" I'm invigorated in my spirit and say, "I knew You had to be listening to the pondering thoughts of the mind of my spirit."

He continues, "And to answer your thought about all of Us being here, the answer is another 'yes.' You spoke it. I'm the Companion and Guide. Jesus is the peace you are walking on and in. The Father is your Almighty Covering.

"You can look at your weapons as tools for warfare. Through the love of the Father, you will know which tool or weapon to use. Proper use of a tool or weapon will bring a proper outcome.

"Not only is your praise a weapon. His love is a weapon, and the peace of Jesus is a weapon. These weapons, as you referred to in scripture, are not carnal, but they are mighty to the pulling down of strongholds. Most times mankind fails to remember that his ways are not Our ways. In the warfare realm one must battle, constantly focused on Our ways. Our ways can seem to be nonsense to the carnal or natural mind, will, and emotions. Our ways are seen from eternal perspective, which is and was and forever will be. That's why this is a warfare realm and not a realm of warfare."

At Holy Spirit's pause, I hear a pinging of steel on steel, like the sound of a steel hammer hitting another piece of steel. Looking towards the sound, I see a figure at a distance in front of us. As the hammer pings, sparks flash. As I focus, I realize this is some type of demonic being wielding a hammer at the bridge and the chains.

Holy Spirit interjects, "Remember, I said you would know when you were close to the other side. You are now close. What are you going to do about it?"

I think, "If I had a bow and arrows, I could shoot that enemy being and take it out."

Holy Spirit clears His throat. I defer to Him. He says, "Get out of your mind and back into your spirit. Think with the mind of your spirit. What weapons do you have?"

Lesson time. He's asking what weapons I have.

I think, "Peace, love, praise. Yes, my praise is a weapon."

He says, "Well then?"

At the sight of this demonic being's attempts to take us out as we advance, I squeak out a few words of praise. This gets its attention, and it motions to more demonic beings who come to the being's aid with more hammers. Swinging increases and pinging gets louder.

Holy Spirit says, "Come on. You can do better than that. I've heard you praising in the car when you're alone. I know you can do better."

From deep within me a voice of praise emerges, a voice I didn't know existed.

"That's better," Holy Spirit says.

The group joins in, and we see our praise as a weapon. The demonic beings drop their hammers and cover their ears with their claw-looking hands. They jump up and start to run. This is a marvelous sight of praise in action.

Holy Spirit says, "They have been looking for this bridge for a long time. Through obedience you and the group have caused it to manifest in the warfare realm. They know once you step into this realm with peace as a weapon strapped on your feet, their time is short. This realm has been entered before, but not with praise and peace. The Father's love empowers this praise and peace, and Jesus died for it. It's only a part of what He took back from hell."

I think, "We made it. The trek to the other side, into this realm, is complete. We are here in the warfare realm. Our feet shod with peace are planted in this realm." With this peace, we kick the hammers over the edge as we look around. A foul odor appears and seems to be dissipating in front of us.

Holy Spirit speaks into my spirit, "That's their covering. From here on unless otherwise noted you will be addressing me as H."

"Yessir, H," my spirit says back to Him. Looking at the group, I see they have orders of their own. Two from the group position themselves at the sides of the bridge. They reach within and pull out flaming swords, holding them in front of themselves.

H says, "Sentinels. They will be guarding this side against future attempts to destroy the bridge."

"Whoa," I think, "they were in the group? I wonder who else these people are?"

H says, "Advance team; that's all you need to know. They each have a mission, and they will be heading out now."

Heart to heart, spirit to spirit, I salute them, and they salute me. No words are spoken. They break into smaller groups and disappear into the warfare realm, dispelling the enemy's cover as they go. I look back to the sentinels guarding the bridge and nod. They tip their swords, and I'm back in my library chair.

What started out as an evaluation got me and the group to the other side, with more lessons along the way.

"Bless them, Papa, in their missions. May I see them again, in Your timing."

Holy Spirit whispers, "All in due time. All in due time."

"Please, Papa, help me in my praise to extend Your love through the peace of Jesus. Amen."

PURE BLUE FLAME

With the communion elements beside me on the little table in the library, the spirit realm opens to me. "I bless my spirit to be out front and receive all You have for me today, Papa. Amen."

On my left is a golden plate. The sides turn up slightly and have a short lip that turns up further like little, short walls around its edge. A golden tea kettle also appears, with a loop as its handle.

A right hand appears, but I only see the back of the hand. The index finger goes through the loop and picks up the kettle. The plate is lifted with the kettle. Somehow all this is attached. The loop begins to glow, then the kettle, and then the plate. At the kettle's spout, a small blue flame appears. It is not bright and doesn't appear to shed much light.

"Papa, what are You showing me?"

I hear in my spirit, "This carries a flame. It's filled with the oil from heaven to make it an eternal flame. This flame guides the way in the darkness."

"Humm," I say. "It doesn't seem to shed much light. How can it guide the way?"

I hear, "In total darkness even a small flame gives off enough light to guide the way."

I ask, "Can anybody see this blue flame?" All is quiet and still as I focus on the blue flame. It burns steadily and consistently, with the flame in the perfect shape of a heart. I've not seen a flame make a heart shape before. "Can you explain more, Papa?"

The flame flutters a bit, but the heart doesn't lose its form. I realize the fluttering was made in the flame by the appearance of Holy Spirit. I feel my body flutter also at His presence.

H says, "Your body didn't lose its form when it fluttered upon Me showing up. Why should the flame?"

I respond, "All flames I have ever seen seem to change form and even extinguish when a slight breeze or wind blows on them, like You showing up. Is it the oil that makes this flame different?"

"It's a combination of things," H says. "First there is the gold. This gold is the purest type of gold. Also, like the gold, the oil from heaven is pure. The shape of the pan, which you are calling a plate, holds the vessel, which you are calling a kettle. Good choice of words by the way. In the natural it does resemble a kettle. Except a kettle is usually used for wet liquid, not burning liquid, oil from heaven.

"A vessel is something that carries something else. Vessels can be large like a ship carrying a big load or small like a thimble carrying a little. In this case Our vessel of oil carries the perfect amount for the flame and task at hand. What you called the spout on the side We call a directional indicator. It points the flame where it's needed. And, yes, the loop, as you called it, is a transmitter. The transmitter receives power from the hand of the one bearing it, in this case the Lord. It then travels through the gold, causing the oil to stir to produce the directional flame that shows the love of the Father, the blue heart flame. But to simplify things, let's just call this a lamp."

I say, "Thank You. My head was spinning at all the explanation You were giving. A lamp is much easier to comprehend."

H responds, "There is wisdom in the Father's design of the lamp and how He made it. Let's break it down a little further. If wisdom has been with Him, the Master craftsman, before there was time, then everything about the lamp is pure, built by pure wisdom from pure wisdom. The gold, the oil, and the flame are all the purest forms."

"This is all wonderful and amazing. Why did Papa show me this? Why such a detailed explanation?"

Holy Spirit gets excited at my question and starts to explain the use of the lamp.

"Watch this," H says, and blows on the flame. His breath causes the flame to grow and brighten like a clear blue sky on a sunny day.

H says, "The blue reflects the light of the Lord."

The flame resumes its form on the lamp. Then He tips the lamp and pours out the oil. The flame follows the oil as it hits the ground and burns on the ground. He moves the lamp and continues to pour the flame. It creates a lighted path in front of me. As He tips the lamp upright, a small drop of burning oil is caught by the pan connected to the bottom of the lamp. Then somehow the flaming oil is absorbed back into the lamp.

H continues, "There are many more uses for this lamp in the warfare realm. The purity of this lamp, its design, its gold, its oil, and its flame are true weapons for Our people sent into that realm. Just like the sentinels at the bridge holding the flaming swords, there are people assigned to carry the lamps. They will carry them and guard them with their lives. They will still be covered with the sheath of praise. They will have the love of the Father and the peace of Jesus in their walk and be covered by the Almighty. They will walk as light bearers with praise as a weapon. They will move in peace with His covering."

"Wow," I exclaim. "This is amazing. Can I ask another question?"

"By all means," H says, chuckling. "Fire away."

I get a big grin at His humor. Holy Spirit is in rare form today. I ask, "If they are light bearers and carrying the lamp in the darkness of the warfare realm, will they draw attention to themselves?"

"Great question," H replies. "You began by seeing a form of a kettle and loop and plate. I thought it would be good for you to see this form of Me." Then He chuckles again.

I grin and laugh. H continues.

"That would be a no and a yes. I said no first because the blue light is not seen by the demonic entities in this realm. They see red or orange. White and bright yellow light blind them. Their eyes are tuned to see these kinds of light, and they turn and run at bright yellow or white. It puts them on notification of their eternal destiny."

H pauses. I put my index finger in the air to ask another question. "Before You answer the yes part, may I?"

"Go right ahead," H replies.

I ask, "Why not just blast this realm with the bright yellow or white light and be done with them?"

"Another good question, and I will address it. As Our light bearers, the carriers of the lamp, have infiltrated and taken their rightful places in this realm, We will turn up the flame. The blue flame, when turned up, will go through stages of orange that look red. Then the fringes of the flame will get so bright it will give the appearance of yellow and bright white.

"This will do two things. It will draw them out and also expose those in the darkness. Their eyes will turn red. By the time this happens, they will be so blinded by the light, they won't be able to see to run. Just as you saw praise as a weapon, light in this realm is a weapon also. Does this answer your question?"

"Yes, it does," I answer. "And generates another."

"I'm all ears," H says.

"Will there be a lot of light bearers? And are they on their way? I guess I generated a two-part question."

"Two parts are good. A question within a question is good with Me," H says. "Light bearers are not counted because they carry something the Father can magnify. Remember Gideon and the 300 torches?"

I nod.

H doesn't miss a beat and continues. "The enemy's camp thought thousands were surrounding them. So, numbers are insignificant with Our magnification. Part two. Yes, some have already been deployed. There were some on the bridge with you and some in the first group after you. A few more since and more in training to come."

"Wow. More groups have come in?" I ask.

H nods and doesn't say a word. Now I continue, "I'm beginning to see man's ways are not Your ways in warfare. Your plan is not annihilation as much as it is occupation."

"Yes," H says. "You are seeing rightly. First of all, the warfare realm was not designed for the enemy. He has occupied a place that is not his to occupy. Sin gave him access, and he still thinks it's his. There are places of occupation for every creature. Even hell has been created for the devil and the fallen angels. That's their place of occupation."

Then H says, "So let's do a little review. When I say, 'My praise,' you say?" H points at me.

I say back to Him, "Is a weapon."

H goes again, "When I say 'sheath,'" as H glows and points, "You say?"

I say back, "Strapped on with the love of the Father."

H again, "When I say 'walk,' You say?" as He points to my feet.

My response is, "In the peace of Jesus."

Now I point and say, "All this is covered by," we say in unison, "God Almighty."

Then H says, "First it's blue," and points to me.

I say, "Then it's red."

H says, "Or orange."

Back to me, "Yellow."

And we both put our hands in the air and point up like to the sun and say, "Bright, blinding white."

H says, "You did well. You're catching on."

I tear up in gratitude and say, "This is a fun way to learn."

"Yes, it is. Yes, it is," H says. "And with that, you meditate on Our lesson for today. There is more to come."

As quickly as that, I'm back in my chair by my little table in the library. I realize a lot is illuminated from a little blue heart-shaped flame.

"Help me, Papa, help me. Amen."

IMPARTATION

As I sit quietly in my library chair praising Papa, the unexpected happens. For the most part, everything that happens in my time with Him, Holy Spirit, and Jesus contains the unexpected.

I didn't expect to be back at the bridge in the warfare realm this morning. I'm not standing in the realm. I'm floating above the valley the bridge spans. I watch the sentinels. I float over to their right side as they face into the darkness of this realm. They both glance at me as I float over, and they tip their swords. All I do is nod and place my hand on my heart.

"What am I doing here, Papa?"

A whoosh of a wind circles about me, and I'm encapsulated by the presence of Holy Spirit. The feeling of floating is one thing, but floating in the presence of Holy Spirit is something totally different. I feel like I'm protected from any outside force that may come against me, and at the same time, I feel part of where I am. I see the two sentinels lower their swords and bow at the waist, honoring His presence. I remember in this realm I'm to refer to Him as H.

In all this, H says, "Good morning. Great to be here with you today."

I'm totally overcome by Him saying it's great to be with me, and I respond, "The pleasure is all mine. What's happening here today?"

He says, "We wanted you to see the entry."

"The entry?" I inquire.

"Yes," H says. "Watch the bridge and the sentinels."

I focus through His presence to watch. Everything seems to be magnified. I see a third man approach the sentinels, coming from the warfare realm. I look intently at him and notice this is the man who was by my side as we crossed over. He turns to acknowledge H with a bow and his right hand placed on his heart. I watch, and he doesn't remove his hand.

H nudges me to salute and says, "He's waiting on you to acknowledge his salute."

"Waiting on me?" I think back to H.

"Yes, you are in My presence, and My presence is what he is saluting. You must salute in return."

I place my right hand over my heart and feel something on my chest. "What's this?" I think back to H.

H responds. "It's a weapon he needs, from the place of the Father's heart. Remove your hand and impart it to him."

I focus on the man. I remove my hand from my heart and turn it toward him. He drops his hand from his heart. I see my hand lying on his heart where his hand was while I'm still in H's presence. "How does this happen?" I wonder.

All H says back to me is, "Our ways, not yours. Impart what you have."

I don't speak audibly, but in the spirit I proclaim, "Receive what I have for you from the Father's heart. May it grow and expand into all you need from Him. Receive it. Amen."

Electricity flows from H and His presence into my heart. A stirring generates and flows through my heart through my extended arm and manifests in my hand on the man's chest. He jerks, and his heart area begins to glow under my hand. All the while the sentinels have their swords lowered and are bowing at the waist. The man receives what I have imparted and seems to stand at attention, taller and more erect.

I remove my hand. The sentinels raise their swords and stand at attention also. The man then nods to them, and they cross their swords to cover the access to the bridge. All this is done with no verbal commands or words. It's all heart to heart, spirit to spirit. I watch in amazement.

H is quick to say, "You're not just watching. You have imparted another weapon to the man from the heart of the Father. You are involved in this process from His, Papa's, heart to the man's heart. Papa used your heart to impart His heart to the other man."

This overwhelms me, and I begin to spin while I float in His presence. H grabs me and pulls me into Himself. In the arms of His presence, I feel a pulsating power fill me to the core.

"In Us you live and move and have your being," He speaks into my spirit. "Your life is in Us. You impart Our life that We have imparted to you."

Through the filling of this impartation, He turns my head towards the bridge. I float with Him above the bridge, His arm around my shoulder, and I feel like a son standing with a proud Papa. Tears of joy, peace, and love flow from my eyes, only to be caught by His hand under my chin.

Then he says, "We, you and I, got this."

More tears flow at His comment. The love is overwhelming.

He nods towards the bridge and says into my spirit, "We didn't want you to miss this."

I see movement on the bridge; I feel excitement in my spirit. The movement is caused by people cautiously moving towards the crossed swords. I count maybe 15 people in a group moving as one. They stop at the swords. The man to whom I gave the impartation studies them very carefully and then motions to the sentinels. They raise their swords.

H says, "They are guarding both ways. Only the mature gain access. Those who move from the Father's heart are the ones we are bringing into the warfare realm. They don't create their own warfare in the realm.

Remember it's not a realm of warfare."

The man receives the group with open arms. The sentinels touch each person's feet with the tips of their swords, causing the glowing peace to be imparted before they enter. The man holds out his right hand, palm towards them, and each one receives a sheath. Then I see it strapped on with the love of the Father.

H says, "He's imparting what he received." I feel a pat on my shoulder from His hand and arm still around me. Needless to say, more tears flow.

Then the group is off on their assignments. They break up into smaller teams to infiltrate the warfare realm.

H says, "More are coming. We wanted you to be part of welcoming the first to come. Thank you."

I'm a clump of a mess. How does one respond to Holy Spirit saying thank you? Another pat on my shoulder, and I float back to my library chair. Double, no triple, whoooa. What a way to start the day.

I hear a chuckle, and H says, "We feel the same."

Sitting quietly in my chair, I still feel like my body's floating as my spirit descends back into my body.

Peace, joy, and overwhelming love flood my being. I see that when we receive an impartation, it's not for us to keep. It's for us to impart.

"Help me, Papa, to be a transmitter of this today. Amen."

ADDED WEAPONS

While praising Papa this morning from my library chair, I sense He is taking me back to the warfare realm. All around me is a dark fog. I hear noises coming from the fog, but I see nothing. The noises are sounds of grunting and of shuffling feet moving along. I hear a whip crack and then the heavy rattle of a chain. These sounds are all around me. I feel uneasy but not fearful.

Then, I feel a presence next to me, and I am filled with peace. The peace comes up from my feet into my legs and flows through my torso into my head. I look down and see my feet glowing from the gold of His peace strapped under and on them. Next to my feet is another pair of feet also shod and strapped with the gold of His peace.

I hear, "One must not walk alone in this realm. I knew when Holy Spirit brought you in. I felt the change. The disturbance you brought in with you also caused the chains of bondage to rattle and the whip to crack." The voice I hear in my spirit is calm and peaceful, coming from the man who was next to me on the bridge.

Through the spirit I say back to him, "I saw you come out of the darkness to the bridge to bring more in. You looked to be alone. I didn't see anyone else with you."

Spirit to spirit he explains, "First, you are wise not to speak audibly. A time will come for that but not yet. You have learned well, and I'm here to help you learn more. I have an eternal companion by my side."

"My name is Knowledge."

With my body trembling, I realize this is one of the seven Spirits of the Lord manifesting next to me. My thoughts go to Isaiah 11:2:

The Spirit of the LORD shall rest upon Him,

The Spirit of wisdom and understanding,

The Spirit of counsel and might,

The Spirit of knowledge and of the fear of the LORD.

My body trembles more at this verse being rehearsed in my mind. I ask, "If you are Knowledge, then Your eternal companion must be the Fear of the Lord."

He nods in agreement and says, "But it's more than that."

"More?" I think.

As He nods and speaks, I hear something in the natural I haven't heard in a while. An owl hoots only once in the woods outside our cottage.

He continues, "You must go further into the book of Isaiah to 33:6:

Wisdom and knowledge will be the stability of your times,

And the strength of salvation;

The fear of the LORD is His treasure.

I feel something move in my chest. I look down to see a scroll coming out of my chest. I put my hands up to grab the sides of the scroll as it continues to automatically roll out of my chest. "What's happening here?" I ask.

"I will defer to Him."

The "Him" he defers to is H. In past encounters, Holy Spirit allowed me to refer to Him as H. It was easier for quick communication in some of what we were doing.

H says to me, "Another weapon."

I respond, "I'm glad You are here. Can You give me understanding?" As I speak, I realize I asked for another one of the seven Spirits, and instantly another Person manifests next to me. I feel reverence and holiness cover me like a heavy blanket. I know it's the Fear of the Lord around me.

H continues, "Your thoughts manifest the next weapon within you. The scroll you hold in your hands is the book of Isaiah. When the living Word of God naturally rolls out of your heart, it is a weapon in your hands. When the Word rolls out of the heart and is quoted from memory, it is used rightly. It brings freedom and healing. It is a pure manifestation through your heart to your hands to those who need it. It also cuts the bondages binding Our people in this realm."

We pause for me to contemplate and comprehend this moment. Then H continues, "We have more for you. We sent the Spirit of Knowledge, and it was good for you to ask for Understanding, because they go hand in hand. One must realize the seven Spirits are of the Lord and are just like Us, the Trinity. When one is manifesting and present, the others are very close by. We sent Knowledge to bring more of what you need to know. You asked for something nearby, in this case by His side, which is Understanding. The owl, guided by Us to hoot at the very same time in the natural, was letting you know Wisdom was at hand to bring Knowledge and give Understanding through the Fear of the Lord.

"In your natural mind you're asking, 'What about Counsel and Might?' They are here but will not manifest now. They will in due time.

"The facets of the Spirit of the Lord work in tandem with each other but also work in unison with each other. One supports another or, at different times, more than one supporting one. They work in unison as well as in tandem. For the Word of God to work rightly, it must always be released in the Fear of the Lord. When it's released in this manner, it's not just a good idea supported by the Word. It's the Word being released, and it supports itself.

"In this realm, function determines form, not the other way around. You see, when Knowledge is released, Wisdom releases Understanding.

True Understanding always comes from the presence of the Lord. The true presence of the Lord is always accompanied by the genuine Fear of the Lord.

"Let's put this knowledge to practice."

"To practice?" I ask. "How do we do that? "

"Great question. Let's bring Understanding in to answer."

"Ok," I respond.

H motions to Understanding, and Understanding speaks Spirit to spirit with me. "What do you have as a weapon that you already use?"

I respond, "My praise?"

"Yes," Understanding replies and then asks, "And how is this used as a weapon?"

I feel H's hand on my mouth, and He whispers, "You were going to praise out loud."

He looks to Understanding and says, "He's got this one. Let's move on to the next."

Knowledge then says, "You already have Understanding about what your words do in this realm."

I nod and respond, "They change the atmosphere. I was excited about praise, and H covered me before I spoke it out."

"Yes, We know," Knowledge says, smiling. Then He asks, "What did I tell you when you arrived?"

"You said You felt my presence enter this realm," I answer.

"True, but let's bring Understanding into that," and Knowledge motions to Understanding.

At this point Understanding speaks up, "Because you are an anomaly to the enemy in this realm, the atmosphere changed. That's why the chains rattled and the whip cracked. If the enemy can feel the change, so can those he controls. He doesn't know why it has changed but doesn't want those he's controlling to be influenced by it. Through Wisdom you will gain Knowledge," nodding to both of them, "of a plan of Wisdom that will bring Me, Understanding, to and for you to move in this realm. This is how the enemy is defeated here. People are rescued and ground is also recovered."

Through Understanding speaking to me, I feel my spirit comprehends all this.

H says, "This is how to operate with Knowledge and any of the other seven Spirits of the Lord. The key is to realize They are with you to work together to bring victory for the Lord."

Understanding speaks up and says, "You know the battle is the Lord's. The victory is His and He gives the increase, right?"

"Yes," I say. "This is common knowledge." Knowledge smiles and nods.

He continues, "I bring Understanding of that knowledge, with Wisdom working it out."

"Wow, this is a simple way to see how all of You work together."

H adds, "All this is possible when a yielded, willing vessel releases the truth of the Word from his heart. Knowledge will be your companion in this realm, but you now know the others are here as well. They are all weapons from the Father's heart through yours. Continue to meditate on this and how you have access to this."

At this statement, I feel the chair under me and know I'm back in the natural--back with Knowledge, Understanding, and Wisdom through the Fear of the Lord in my sheath.

With joy in my spirit, I say,

"Thanks, Papa. Help me to use all these weapons rightly. Amen."

UNDERSTANDING COMES

While I sit in my library chair this morning, I think about the events of my last visit to the warfare realm. "Are the seven Spirits of the Lord that close? Are they accessible to us as believers at any time?"

In my inquiry, my natural mind seems to somehow connect with my spirit in a new way. There isn't the separation I've felt in the past of a questioning natural mind and a believing mind of the spirit. Holy Spirit said these weapons were manifesting in that realm, but is that realm about us all the time?

"Holy Spirit, I need Knowledge and Understanding through Wisdom operating through the Fear of the Lord. I want to be in proper alignment. Can I just ask for them to come, or do You send them?"

I sit quietly and wait. The air in the room seems to clean itself. Things in front of me seem crystal clear. Next, I see a chasm in front of me with two different types of land masses on either side. I don't see the bottom of the separation between the two, just an endless view into nothingness. Then a semitransparent tubular structure starts to appear from left to right and connects the two land masses. The finished structure looks like an arch from one place to the other. The semitransparent material glows and moves and reflects its surroundings.

Then, on the opposite side of the arch from me two big eyes appear, looking at me. I'm startled but somehow feel the arch is a barrier between me and these eyes. As I focus on the eyes, I see the area around the pupils, the iris, spin and get wider, then smaller. The eyes focus on me as I do the same to them. Then a nose and face appear, then a furry, tan skin, then a fluffy mane. This is the Lion of the tribe of Judah! When I recognize Him, He turns and walks a short distance away from the arch. He is walking on nothing above the chasm between the land masses. He wags His tail, turns, and sits, again on nothing, He looks at me through the arch.

I sit, amazed. I ask, "Papa, can You please give me understanding of all this?"

I feel a whoosh around me. I realize Understanding just showed up, with Knowledge by Her side. My inner being stirs. Good thing I'm sitting, or this might have knocked me over. I feel Their presence, but at the same time I feel I need to ask for Their input. Peace like a river fills me. I take a deep breath and release it. Holy Spirit says, "Good morning."

Before I can even answer, They answer Him with a "good morning" in return.

"Whoa, They're on it," I think. With chuckling all around, I say good morning to Them. They return the greeting.

Holy Spirit says, "You asked for Them to come. What's on your mind?"

I pause and realize I will most likely get more than I ask but don't want to ask amiss.

Understanding chimes in, "No wrong questions here. We have all the time you need."

"Are the others here?" I ask.

Knowledge says, "Let me ask you a question."

Surprised, I think, "The Spirit of Knowledge wants to ask me a question?" I sit up straighter in my chair. "Ok," I respond, "I believe I'm ready. Shoot."

"When Holy Spirit told you We were like the Trinity, did you believe Him?"

I stutter, "Yes, I believed Him. My question was more for a point of reference."

Suddenly, I hear clicking of heels on a hard-surfaced floor, and the room is filled with a pleasant fragrance.

A male voice speaks, "Now, now, don't be too hard on him. He is new at this. I know you ruffle my feathers from time to time, but I'm used to it. He is still moving back and forth and living more in the natural than the spiritual."

I feel a pat on my back, and joy floods my being.

Enoch says to me, "Just go with it. Remember that ultimate true Knowledge, looking at Him, knows everything and wants to reveal it."

Knowledge nods.

Enoch continues, "He will reveal it, but lean into Understanding and remember you have eternity to learn. Stay focused on what the Lord has at hand for you right now. And, yes, They all are here and will chime in as needed." With that, Enoch turns and says, "Well, guys, see ya later."

I'm so overwhelmed I don't even say a word. I just watch him disappear as quickly as he showed up. I sit in a state of wonder. I put my hands on my face and remember I need to get ready for church. I'll be back.

It's evening, and I'm back.

I hear Understanding clear Her throat. I'm back in Their presence.

I take another deep breath and focus on Them. I sit up straighter again and ask, "What is the meaning of the two land masses, the chasm, and the connection tube between them? What's the tube made from, and what's its purpose? Is there a reason the Lion of the tribe of Judah is here?"

Whoa. I take another deep breath and think, "That was like rapid fire."

Holy Spirit smiles and defers to Knowledge. He unfolds his arms, leans towards me, and begins. "Let's go back a little further. We cleared the air for you to see and hear clearly."

"Yes," I say. "Thanks for doing that. Is that why I felt no separation between the natural questioning mind and believing in the spiritual?"

He answers, "Yes, but there is more."

He nods to Understanding who says, "Great questions. We brought clarity for you to see and hear more clearly, even though you live more in the natural realm, as Enoch said. One of Our best students," and She nods to Knowledge.

Knowledge nods back and says, "Yes, one of the best."

Then Understanding continues, "It's good for you to think about the spiritual from the natural mind. You created the atmosphere for Us to work in. You asked about Us being close and around you. We need to cover a few more things to answer the question about the warfare realm being around you.

"Let's get back to the atmosphere. Inquiring about Us being near you opened your spirit to receive from the spiritual realm. Your focus on Us cleared the air for pure Understanding to be released. It gave way to the Spirit of the Lord to release Us to come. You sealed the space by asking the Father to send us.

"The Lion is here on guard, preventing any access from the second heaven. He focused in on you, and you focused on His eyes. Because your focus was pure and not fearful, He revealed the rest of Himself and showed you He is watching." Understanding nods back to Knowledge, and says, "Your turn."

I focus on Knowledge, and He says, "The two land masses are the natural and the spiritual realms." He points and says, "You need to get this. Understanding is here for more clarity if need be. The masses, as you call them, are not places as you would think they are. They are realms, not locations. They are dimensional. The chasm between them will always be there. The nothingness in between is where a lot of people stop. They want to move into a deeper relationship with the Father, Son, and Holy Spirit, but when they experience nothing, they go back to what they know, what is familiar.

"The separation is there for two reasons: to keep the two separate and to provide testing to continue in Him even if one feels nothing. But you have learned that in the nothing, He is there, and He is everything in nothing. This is a big learning point for many people. Even very committed, strong believers are stumped with that one."

"Trying to figure it out without coming to us through the Lord will keep people stumped," Understanding chimes in.

Knowledge continues, "We work with Holy Spirit in all your lessons and will be with Him and you through eternity. Your turn." He points back to Understanding.

This time Understanding opens with a question, "So why do you think we have been taking you through these lessons?"

I answer with my first thought, "Because of my desire to know Jesus on a more intimate level."

"Yes," She says back to me. "Your deep desire to know Him has brought about all these lessons. These eternal lessons will forever be unfolding in your spirit. Life is eternal, and a lifelong learner is an eternal learner.

"The reason for the tunnel of life, the semitransparent tube-like connection between the two land masses, the two realms, is for you and those who move back and forth to have safe passage. This is the way you have moved back and forth. It's not a matter of your doing this on your own. The tunnel is built by the Father through Wisdom to provide safe passage. You felt this as you moved back and forth. You just didn't know what it was. As a matter of fact, as you see this, you are in this at the same time. It's not a matter of fighting your way through. It's a matter of leaning in--like John the beloved disciple demonstrated in his book, 13:23-25,

Now there was leaning on Jesus' bosom one of His disciples, whom Jesus loved. Simon Peter therefore motioned to him to ask who it was of whom He spoke.

Then, leaning back on Jesus' breast, he said to Him, "Lord, who is it?"

"As he leaned on Him, wanting to get close to the heart of Jesus, the Lord answered him in his closeness. When he leaned in, he could ask Him the most intimate question of His betrayal and betrayer.

"Through this closeness you move from the natural to the spiritual naturally. Do you see now why We needed the air clear?"

I nod in the affirmative, my mind reeling. I'm still blown away at the conversation and the closeness of the Spirit of Understanding and Knowledge through the Fear of the Lord.

Understanding says, "Seems like you're drifting? Does this bring clarity and understanding to your questions?"

I apologize and respond, "Yes, it is, but I'm on overload and still trying to comprehend I'm even having this conversation."

Understanding says, "I understand, but the good thing is, you are having this conversation, and you're having it with Us and not trying to figure all this out on your own."

"Good point," Knowledge says, "I know how you feel also. You should hear some of the things I hear about how people are in the know."

I smile.

He says, "Good. I thought that would lighten things up. What do you think, Holy Spirit? Should we put him to bed with this for now and let him sleep on it?"

Holy Spirit responds in the affirmative by wrapping me in His presence like a warm blanket. "Yes. We'll let him sleep on this. After all, we have eternity together."

I know I never left my chair in the natural but have been with Them in the spiritual. And with all this information, there is even more of a clarity in the air about me. Knowing that, I'll sleep well tonight. I breathe in deeply and exhale two words, "Thank You."

In the quietness and peace, They leave me, and I prayerfully head to bed.

"Please, Papa, speak to me more about this in the night. Amen."

ARROW AND LIGHT

After sitting several minutes in my library chair in our cottage in the woods, my praise to Him is pleasantly interrupted by the spirit realm opening to me. With my eyes closed, I see a moving arrow in front of me. I grab my iPad, open my eyes, and type what I'm seeing.

The arrow is flat and black, and the background is a light gray color. The tail of the arrow seems to be connected at the end to something, and the point moves from pointing up and then to the right and back up again. The tail of the arrow doesn't slide to the right. It bends. The tail of the arrow seems to be spring loaded to go back up after it bends to the right.

The arrow continues its movement, and I see a spinning light coming from behind the arrow. The light seems to have a head or a small round point on it to direct it and a tail of light behind it. As the light spins, it rotates like a corkscrew. Sparks of light seem to break off the light and disappear in the air around it as it continues to come towards the arrow. The light gains speed the closer it gets to the arrow.

The arrow continues in its methodical motion, from up, to the right, and back again. From the back of the arrow at the connection point, I see something start to grow towards the incoming light. The form that's growing looks like a baseball catcher's mitt ready to catch a perfect pitch.

Questions form in my mind, but I don't speak them out. I continue to wait and focus on the unfolding scene in front of me. There is no sound in all of this, only sight. I think, "Papa, thank You for giving me eyes to see. Please clarify my vision and tune my ears to hear."

Everything stops in front of me and moves in reverse. There is still no sound, only reverse motion of what I saw.

Then, I'm back at the beginning, and the arrow is moving. It goes up, then to the right. I hear a loud ticking sound like a clock every time the arrow moves to the right. Then there's a boing sound like a metal spring bouncing back to the upright position. This continues, a click and a boing, a click and a boing.

Then I hear a sound like a fireworks rocket and see light coming towards the moving arrow. The sparks crackle, flare, and disappear.

I hear in my spirit, "You asked for sight and sound, and you got it."

"Thanks, Papa," I think, "I'm learning not to just assume but to continue to ask You to let me see and hear."

Back to the arrow and the light. Next I hear a sound like a thick rubber balloon expanding. The expansion forms a catcher's mitt. "Papa," I think, "the sound makes this exciting. I can actually feel the sounds as I hear them."

Then a rush of wind comes from behind me. A cool chill causes me to tremble and wiggle. I say, "Good morning, Holy Spirit. Thanks for coming today."

I hear back from Him, "My pleasure."

I ask, "Are You here to give me understanding?"

"Not yet," He replies. "The Father sent Me to interject something."

"I'm all ears," I say. Meanwhile I continue to hear the click and boing, the crackling flare and sparks, and the expansion of the mitt.

He says, "You are seeing, hearing, and feeling the way you were created to see and hear and feel."

As He says this, I can see, hear, and feel His words swirl and swoosh around me, even in the midst of the other sounds coming from the arrow scene.

He continues, "Mankind has shut down their senses to only hear or only see or only feel. Living is a multifaceted, multifunctional, multidimensional experience a lot of people are missing out on. Why? Because they relegate life to one or, at the most, two natural sensing actions. I have Understanding here to explain."

"Good morning, Understanding," I say. I see a spirit-like cloud appear coming out of Holy Spirit and feel Their multiple presence.

Understanding speaks, "When people are outside on a cold day, they can hear their words, see their breath, and feel their body shiver as it experiences the cold air. These are the senses of mankind, created to give mankind a multidimensional, experiential life. But most people will not pay attention to their words they hear and their breath they see. They will say, without seeing and hearing or feeling, 'I'm cold. I'm going in where it's warm.'

"You are learning to experience life the way the Father intended for it to be experienced. There are times when one needs to shut down the seeing, hearing, or feeling, but from our perspective it's not a long-term recommendation. We can temporarily dull hearing to give better vision. Or temporarily cloud the vision to give clearer hearing. We do this to make a point. The feelings are all yours. The Father in His wisdom has relegated and confined your feelings, the feelings of mankind, to them.

"While I'm here, I'll answer the question in your mind. But first let Me say, that question is there not because you're distracted but because you're functioning multidimensionally. The Father will continue to unfold the vision He started in front of you, and We will bring clarity. He wanted you to have this lesson on the multifaceted, multifunctional, multidimensional aspects of life. We will be back later, but for now let's get back to the vision."

Just as I saw in the spirit how Understanding came out of Holy Spirit, I see Her go back in. But Her words are reverberating through my spirit. I'm excited to get back to the vision Papa put on pause for Them to allow me see and hear and feel Them speak.

I ask, "In this pause, Papa, can I divert to the communion elements and get ready for church?"

I hear back, "All in all," and my body shudders. I take this as permission to pause. I know I'll be back later for the continuation of this vision lesson.

CLASSROOM

This morning, I see in front of me a big book being opened. I stand behind the person who is opening the book. I realize the person is a female, and she sits at a desk like a teacher. The hard-covered book looks old. Not ancient, just old, but not used much and not well cared for. I don't see full pages, only the cover being opened and the upper right corner of a blank page. The cover is old gold leaf color, and the color even flows to the inside of the cover.

I don't feel myself move, but I find myself standing at the back of a room looking over students' heads towards the person who opened the book. This is a classroom with a female teacher. It's an old room with a big black chalk board behind the teacher. The alphabet is pasted across the top of the chalk board. The letters in the alphabet are printed capital and lower case on the top and cursive capital and lower-case letters below each letter.

I feel to look behind me.

When I do, I see another group of letters of some sort. I can't read them, but the way they are lined up on the wall gives me the impression they, too, represent an alphabet. Turning back towards the teacher, I see a few windows on the sides of the room, but no light comes in from them. Although the room is totally illuminated with natural light, I do not see any lights in the room.

Students of different ages all face the teacher and seem attentive, younger students in front and older students in the back. I sense excitement in the room. The teacher, a young woman with long brown hair pulled back on one side, looks up from the book at the students and says, "Story time."

When she says this, the room erupts into what I first think is chaos. I hear chairs sliding on a wooded floor, a few giggles, and some talking. The desks are moved to the edges of the room. The older students either move towards the younger ones or sit next to them in the chairs they moved. A few even put the young ones on their laps. What looked like chaos turns into a group of students quietly sitting in a semi-circle in front of the big blackboard. The teacher's desk is now moved to the left, and the teacher sits in her chair next to her desk in front of the students. The big book is open on her lap.

All is quiet in the room except for a click, a boing, and the sound of a flaming rocket crackling.

The teacher says, "We will continue where we left off yesterday."

I think, "Papa, is this a continuation of where You left off yesterday? Is the teacher the Spirit of Wisdom?"

A presence next to me makes my body tremble in a good way. I know Holy Spirit has entered the room. I see Him swirl around the students and encapsulate them in His presence. As He does this, the students seem to sit up straighter as if their attention has been heightened by His presence. Even the light in the room gets brighter. I look at the windows. Still, no natural light comes through them. This entire room is illuminated by a holy presence. I can feel it and see it.

The click, boing, and crackling sounds are still there.

I move to a chair next to the students to listen to the story. The students don't see me as an outsider. I'm just part of the class and fit right in with them. I even feel like I'm part of the student body in this classroom. My age doesn't seem to make any difference. I even feel a heightened sense of attentiveness in my spirit. It hits me--this is a spirit classroom.

I feel Holy Spirit get close to me and whisper, "Yes, this is a spirit class, and there are many students of varying natural ages in the class." I do a quick look around to see young children through middle-aged adults, and even a few with full silver heads of hair.

He continues, "In the spirit, age makes no difference. When someone is learning Spirit to spirit, the spirit is being taught to lead the soul and the body. This is not head knowledge. This is the Spirit of Wisdom, bringing the Spirit of Understanding, with the Spirit of Knowledge confirming the lesson in their spirits and in your spirit. There is no age difference in the spirit. The natural mind of man has limited the spirit to its capacity in the mind of man. Let's listen to what the Spirit of Wisdom has to say."

She says, "Remember through the reverent and holy Fear of the Lord."

At her first statement, the room fills with a holiness that rests upon us and causes us all to bow and then lift our heads in this presence.

She continues, "We can learn what He has for us in the spirit."

Then she looks at me. Her deep, sky-blue eyes penetrate my spirit. I feel Holy Spirit's hand on my back, as if holding me up.

She says, "This reverent fear of the Lord is like a weapon next to our hearts that wraps the love of the Father around us. This is the first and the key to all the spiritual weapons He has for each of us."

I ask from my spirit, "Is this a training class for teams who will enter the warfare realm?"

She doesn't hesitate in her speaking but nods in the affirmative at me. I think, "Whoa, talk about multi-tasking! She is doing it in the spirit." I see a smile and another nod, and she directs her attention to the other students. My spirit comes to attention. It's ready to receive from the Spirit of Wisdom in this part of an unfolding eternal lesson.

The clicking and boing don't seem to miss a beat.

She says, "The light of the rocket is coming in."

At her words, the big blackboard changes into a swirling cloud, and the rocket of light heads towards us. I hear gasps in the room. The older students who have younger students on their laps hug them in reassurance the rocket won't hit them. I even feel an affirming pat on my back from Holy Spirit, and my heart rate comes back to normal. Everything is so real in front of me that I feel I can reach out and touch it.

Wisdom continues to speak, although her words are coming alive in front of us on the blackboard. The arrow appears in front of the incoming rocket of light. The catcher's mitt is between the arrow and the light, ready for the catch.

Again, everything is put on pause. I look at the clock in the natural, and it's been almost two hours, and I need to get ready for work.

I hear in my spirit, "We'll be back. Stay spirit focused."

"Papa, help me stay spirit-focused while in the natural until You bring me back into the spiritual. Amen."

A FRIEND NAMED SIR

Most of my day yesterday was filled with tasks that didn't take much mental bandwidth. Therefore, I had time to ponder the morning events from the last couple of days.

Sitting in my library chair this morning, I'm overcome by His holiness. I'm so, so thankful to Jesus for what He did on the cross for us. The redemption and access we now have to a holy God, the God of heaven and earth. I proclaim, "You are holy. Yes, You are the God of heaven and earth. Hallelujah."

As I worship Him who Is All in all, I'm moved into the spirit realm.

I know I'm going back to the classroom, but I feel I'm diverted to another place. I feel the warm, covering presence of Holy Spirit next to me as I move through the atmosphere.

He says, "That was a sweet time this morning with you as you were worshiping the Father."

I respond with tears of joy because Holy Spirit is blessed by me and my worship to Papa and all of Them.

He says back to me, "All of heaven rejoices when one person worships. Each single act of worship does not go unnoticed by Us and by all of heaven."

This is a sobering statement. I, in my short time of praise and worship, have touched heaven and, more importantly, Them--Father, Son, and Holy Spirit.

I say, back to Him, "My words really do have power."

He responds, "More than you know or realize. More than you know. You are learning, and there is still more to learn."

As He says this, my thoughts finish His sentence. As I think what He's saying, we both say, "We have eternity to continue to learn about His ways."

"Wow," I think, "I'm beginning to come in sync with Them."

"More than you know. More than you know," He says to my thoughts.

I'm reminded about taking every thought captive and how this adds another level to that teaching.

While I ponder, Holy Spirit says, "We have to make a pick up."

"A pick up?" I inquire.

"Yes," He says, "We have a friend joining the class today, and I told him we would pick him up."

I'm excited about meeting another one of His friends. I must remember not to look on the outside but to look to the spirit. To see and hear with the eyes and ears of my spirit.

He says, "It is good you're thinking with the mind of your spirit and activating your spiritual seeing and hearing. We are almost there to get him."

We pause, and Holy Spirit says, "We are here."

We are in front of a large, solid door. The door looks cold and resembles steel. Even though I'm next to Holy Spirit, I feel cold, and a depressing spirit comes from the door.

He says to me, "We are here. Go ahead and knock. He knows we are coming."

I knock on the door, and, yes, it is steel. The strike of my hand makes a very loud, clanging sound. I step back and hear several bolts unlock. I almost feel as if I'm standing at a prison door. The door slowly creeks open, and a figure of a person appears in the opening. I'm shocked to see a man covered in chains. Chains are around his neck, on his shoulders, around his wrists, and even around his ankles.

But I look past the outer appearance and focus on his spirit. When I see this, I almost vomit. His spirit is just as bound up, except for a very tiny speck of light buried deep beneath the bonds. These bonds resemble chains, but they look dark and heavy.

I feel a pat on my back. I clear my throat and say, "Hi, we are here to pick you up."

Very dark, blood-shot eyes look at me, and he asks, "Is He here? You know, H?"

I find it interesting even though we are in a place of freedom, this man is referring to Holy Spirit only as H.

Holy Spirit is quick to speak into my spirit, "Conditioning. His bonds and chains are keeping him in his bondage. He doesn't trust you yet. Let him know I'm here."

"Why, yes," I say, "He's right here with me."

"Good," he says. "Let me get my coat and hat." He moves slowly, and the heavy chains rattle.

Again, Holy Spirit says into my spirit, "Conditioning. We have time."

The man comes back to the door, wearing a coat woven of chains. The coat hangs down past his waist, and on his head rests a skull cap, also woven of chains. He has a big steel ring of keys in his hand. And he smells like heavy oily steel.

He says, "Ok, I'm ready to go but just need to lock up."

"Whoa, what bondage," I think.

He uses several keys to throw several dead bolts in the door. Interestingly, he hangs the keys on a hook outside of the door.

He looks at me and says, "The ring is too heavy to carry around, so I'll leave them here for when I come back."

I just respond, "Ok, then we are ready to go." I'm not going to address the fact the keys are available to anyone who walks up.

Holy Spirit says, "Keys or no keys, no one in their right mind wants to go in there."

The man says to me, "Feels good out here. It's been a while since I've been out."

"Well, Sir, we better be on our way," I say.

"How did you know my name was Sir?" he asks.

"Lucky guess," I say, shrugging my shoulders at Holy Spirit, Who's right next to us.

"Yeah," he says, "H probably told you. How's He doing? Is He coming with us?"

I respond, "Yes, He is," as I look to H. He has His finger over His lips to keep me from letting Sir know He's here.

I continue, "He provided transportation, and He will meet us there."

I'm thinking, "Talk about spiritual impromptu!"

"Good," Sir responds, "He knows my condition, and I suspect the ride will accommodate me."

"Yes, Sir, accommodation's made," and we both are lifted off the ground.

Sir looks at me and says, "Wow, I feel light. Haven't felt this in a long time. Don't know how to react to this."

I say, "Just go with it. H thought you would like the transport." Again, I shrug my shoulders at H and lift my hands, palms up.

H speaks to my spirit, "You're doing great. He just needs a friend."

I nod at H and then say to Sir, "Quite a coat you got there. I haven't seen one like that before. And the hat is an added touch."

He says, "Yeah, many years of toil to get this beauty. The hat was an extra. Coat fits me real good, still getting used to the hat."

I reflect, "He thinks the coat is good. He must be so set in the bondage he's in that he can't see it for what it is."

H responds to my thoughts, "You're seeing and perceiving correctly. Don't add to the bondage. Keep the conversation light."

When H says the word *light*, I think of the first time I was aware I was meeting with Wisdom. How Wisdom illuminated me on light. Sir and I chit chat on light topics for the rest of our journey to the classroom. Before long, we are there.

I say to Sir, "We are here. Let's go inside."

He says to me, "I am really liking this outside feeling. Do we need to go inside?"

I say, "Yes, we do, but it's light in there, too, and H is in there." He agrees, and we walk through a wooden door into the classroom.

He says, "Yes. Feels nice in here also."

The students make room for us to sit. They don't even stare at him, but Sir hesitates.

I say, "It's okay. There are seats for us over there." He leans over to me and whispers in my ear.

He asks me where his cage is.

My eyes fill with tears at his words.

Wisdom takes over and says, "Good morning, Sir. We have been waiting for you. We couldn't fit that old cage in here, so we just got you a chair. You can leave your coat and hat at the door. You won't need them in here."

Sir hesitantly agrees and begins to remove his coat of chains, then the hat.

"First step," Holy Spirit whispers into my spirit. "Give him a hand."

I reach out to help him remove his coat.

He thanks me by saying, "It's been hard for me to get that coat off. Thanks for the help. And, yes, here's the hat."

I say, "I'll leave them at the door as the teacher said to do." I think I'll just carry the coat and hat to the door, but once off of Sir, I can't pick it up because it's so heavy. The hat alone is heavy enough. It takes everything in me to try to drag the coat. One of the strong, younger male students jumps up and helps me drag it to the door and leave the hat with it.

"Thanks for giving me a hand," I say.

"You're welcome," he says, and we head to our seats. Mine is next to Sir.

Sir leans over and says, "She's young and pretty. Is she old enough to be a teacher?" Then he says, "Is H here?"

I say, "She has wisdom beyond her years. She is qualified. You need to look past the outer appearance. And, yes, H is here. We can visit with Him at a break."

"He scares me," Sir says back. "First time I saw Him, eyes like fire, everyone ran, except me. My condition won't let me run, you know."

"I see," I respond. "He scares me sometimes, too, but it's a good fear. When you get to know Him, you will really like Him. Let's sit back and listen to what she has for us today."

He nods in agreement.

As I lean back in my chair, I feel my library chair replace that of the classroom. I'm back in the natural, my face now dried up from the tears of meeting Sir.

"Please impart wisdom, Papa, and help me with Sir. Amen."

LITTLE GIRL

This morning after getting to my library chair, I spend several minutes in praise, worshiping the King of kings and Lord of lords. Then, I'm moved into the spirit realm.

The rain drops hitting the metal roof on our cottage in the woods bring back the sound of the arrow. I hear a click, and, to my surprise, right on cue, Lisa's laptop across the room makes a sound similar to the boing of the arrow coming back up. This happens twice. I realize I'm in two realms at the same time.

In the spirit realm, I sit in the classroom next to Sir. In the natural, it's still dark outside while I sit in my library chair. I see a flash of light out of the corner of my right eye. Looking in that direction, I only see the fern next to the window.

Then Sir comes into focus, seated to my right. Naturally, he's sitting in the end chair, because it is a chair with no one next to him. He is okay with me sitting in the chair between him and the young man who helped with his coat. But he is still a little uneasy.

Wisdom has called for a short recess. A young girl, maybe seven or eight years of age, pushes a chair across the wooden floor. It doesn't leave any marks, but I hear it scuffing along. She situates the chair next to Sir on his right and jumps up on the chair. I feel uneasiness coming from Sir and hear his chains rattling. I think, "Who is she, and what's going to happen here?"

Holy Spirit comforts my concerns with, "She is following My leading to interact with Sir. You just pray for her and him. Prayer is a big priority when you work with people like Sir in the warfare realm. Focused prayer keeps you in the mind of the spirit, and the natural mind doesn't have space to take over."

I feel an aha moment in my spirit, and years of teaching and learning coming together in my spirit. Focused prayer is directed prayer. Directed prayer comes from Him to hit the specific target.

"Yes, it is," Holy Spirit says.

I pray, "I ask for Your leading, Papa. Tune my ears to hear Your words of prayer for this moment." In my spirit I pray for this time with the little girl and Sir.

She is still a little wiggly on her chair, but I see she has no fear. She looks up at him. He stares at the blackboard in front of us, not paying attention to her.

She says, "Hey, Mr. Sir, it's nice to have you with us today in our class."

Sir still looks straight ahead and acts like she's not there. He even turns his head a little to the left, away from her.

She is persistent, and the next words surprise me as my prayer intensifies for her. Looking around the room, I see others in focused prayer for her as well. I notice this is not just a class of individuals. It's a group of individuals in sync with each other. They are a team.

She doesn't lose her focus on him and says, "I really like your jewelry, Mr. Sir. Where did you get all this bling?"

This gets his attention, and he looks at her sitting next to him.

I think, "This is amazing. The wisdom of this little girl to identify with him through his bondage but not add to it, even though she recognizes it."

He eases up a bit and seems less tense. He turns to look at the girl. Her dark olive skin contrasts with her deep green eyes. She looks up at him, never losing focus while she waits for his answer. She has genuine interest in him and his bling, as she called it.

He says, "Well, I've never looked at this as jewelry or bling," as he grabs a chain draped across his chest.

She says, "Oh, well, what do you call it then?"

I hear a bit of rattling, and his chair moves a little. I feel tension rise up in him again, but the little girl is at peace with all of this and is not being rattled in her spirit. The complexion of her face and deep green eyes looking up at him draw him in and lead him to answer.

After a pause he says, "These were awards given to me for good behavior."

She replies, "Wow, that's something. So, you must be proud of them then. I know when I get an award, I put it on a shelf for others to see, but I never thought of wearing the awards like you have."

He says, "They were placed on me, and I was told they couldn't be taken off."

Again, she replies with words of wisdom. I glance over at Wisdom herself as she stands by her desk and see she is focused on the two of them. I have to believe she is speaking to the little girl Spirit to spirit.

Then the little girl looks at him intently, almost like she's looking right through him, and says, "We have been learning about true rewards. The teacher has told us true rewards are on the inside. They are rewards in our hearts."

Wow, she cut right to the inner bondages in Sir.

He says to her, "My, little lady, you have a way with words."

She says, "Thanks," and jumps off the chair. She comes around in front of him and says, "It's been really great talking to you." She places her hand on one of the chains on his left knee and says, "Maybe one day you can tell me more about your rewards, and we can take one or two off to make room for some others." With that she runs off to play with a friend.

I think, "This is amazing how she approached him, and he didn't seem to get offended."

Sir looks at me and says, "Quite a little girl. She likes my bling."

For the first time, I see a glimmer of hope in his eyes. Maybe this was the quick flash of light I saw manifesting in him earlier. The little girl reminds me of another little girl I met awhile back.

I reply to Sir with, "Yes, seems like she is amazing." I wave my hand across the room and say, "Looks like lots of amazing people here."

He leans over and says, "Yes it does, but where is H? You said He's here. Will I get to see Him?" All the while, Holy Spirit has been behind us like a big brother.

I glance at H, and He says to my spirit, "Tell him, 'All in due time. All in due time.'"

"Yes, Sir, He's here, and we will see Him, all in due time."

Sir repeats, "All in due time. He said that to me before. When all the others ran, and I couldn't. I thought I was done for, but He took me out of the place I was in and brought me to a nicer place. That's where you picked me up."

A quick thought goes through my mind, "Oh my, that was a nicer place?"

Sir continues, "Yup, He said He would be back all in due time. Said something about preparing a place for me all in due time, all in due time, said it twice."

Sir smiles and says, "Man, those eyes of fire. The task masters over me didn't like them. They actually shrieked when they ran. Never thought I would hear that coming from them. They were in total control. That is till H showed up. I thought I was done for, but now I'm here.

"That little girl was sweet, wasn't she?"

I say, "Yes, you are here, and, yes, she was sweet towards you. Maybe we'll meet a few more."

I glance over at Wisdom again and see she is getting ready to continue the class.

The smile on my face broadens. I know Holy Spirit has everything under control. I lean back in my chair and feel it replaced with my library chair. I'm back in the natural.

Wow, what an amazing little girl. The way she followed the leading of Wisdom was a lesson in itself.

"Thank You, Papa, for my small part in this today. Guide me by Wisdom in this day. Amen."

SIR'S DISCERNMENT

As I sit in my library chair this morning, the click and boing of the arrow come back into my spiritual hearing. I feel my chair switch to the classroom chair. In front of me things are coming back into order after recess. All the students are back in their chairs, facing the blackboard. Sir is to my right, and there's an empty chair next to him. I pray in my spirit and have to trust Holy Spirit that Sir will receive what He brought him here to receive.

I think of times in the past when I have invited friends to church or a special meeting, and I was concerned with what the teacher, minister, or speaker would say. It was as if I was being their holy spirit, instead of letting Holy Spirit be who He is.

"Sir is Your friend, and I defer to You, Holy Spirit. Let me receive what I need to receive, and let him receive what You have for him.

"I pray for Sir this morning, Papa. I lift him before You, that he would receive all You have for him. That You, through Wisdom, would break off the bondages he is in and under. That You, through Wisdom and Understanding, would set him free. Amen."

Wisdom is sitting next to her desk with the book on her lap. She asks, "What do you think the light coming in is?"

At her words the blackboard again becomes a movie screen, and the light coming in is magnified. The crackling fire coming in seems brighter.

I hear a slight rattle of chains. It's Sir leaning towards me. He says in a low voice, "I know exactly what that light is."

I say back to him, while staying focused on the board, "You do?"

He says, "Yes. That's the fire coming from the eyes of H. That is what caused the others to run. That is the fire I saw when I met Him. Total darkness around me, not like the light of this room. A dark heavy covering around me and that fire coming from H."

I hear another rattle as Sir lifts his hand and arm to point towards the blackboard. He emphasizes, "That light is the fire that was coming from His eyes."

I think, "This is a tremendous explanation of the light coming in."

I see students' hands raised in the air. Wisdom selects a student on the other side of the room, and we all focus on that person, awaiting his answer. This young man appears to be in his late teens with short black hair and a slender build.

He says, "That is light coming from heaven into the world."

"Good answer," she says back to him and asks, "Who else has an idea of what this is?"

I hear more rattling coming from the seat next to me. I know Sir is being touched by this. I wonder if he is feeling uncomfortable.

At my wondering thoughts, I feel the weight of a hand on my right shoulder. My spirit is filled with peace that calms my wondering about what Sir is thinking.

Holy Spirit then whispers into my spirit. "I have him covered. He will get through this. You continue to be prayerful for him and the others. When one receives in an attentive group like this, all receive. Everyone will receive a different piece of the picture, depending on where they are at naturally and spiritually. All the pieces will come together to make the whole. Pray and listen, not just for them but for yourself also."

My spirit shifts into thankfulness at Holy Spirit's comforting words. I think, "I have been invited to this class also."

I pray, "Papa, please help all of us receive what You have for us to receive. Let Wisdom break through all the bondages holding us back. I give this time to You. Amen." I shift to praying in the Spirit.

Other students have different perspectives of the light coming in. Wisdom always affirms and comforts the students when she responds to them. Then she closes the book, slides it onto her desk, and gets up from her chair. Even when she closes the book, the light coming in still travels on the blackboard and seems to get closer and closer.

Now standing in front of the class, she addresses us by saying, "I know that some of you have been wondering who our special guest is today?" She takes a few steps towards Sir and me, then back towards her chair. She pauses for us to think.

I think, "Is she going to introduce Sir to share about himself? No, she can't do that. He won't say anything. He might just sit there, not saying a word, or just leave."

Then, on the blackboard I see the catcher's-mitt-looking shape behind the arrow. The crackling light is approaching it. A loud pop silences the boing of the arrow going up. The arrow is straight up, and it doesn't go back to the right. The light sizzles in the mitt like a skillet with hot food on it. The atmosphere changes from the impact of the light, or fire as Sir pointed out, hitting the mitt.

Then she says, "Let's all welcome Holy Spirit to take this part of the class." More rattling comes from the chains on Sir. The tension I feel rising next to me causes me to increase the intensity of my prayer.

Being who He Is, a whoosh of wind blows over us and then a cloud-shaped being is standing next to Wisdom. His being is glowing and pulsating. Power is being released from Him. I naturally bow my head and feel like I should prostrate myself on the floor, but the peace permeating the atmosphere is also inviting us into Him.

Chains rattle again, and Sir leans towards me. "Yup, that's Him. Came in the same way to the other class I was in. Except that class didn't have a pretty, smart teacher like this one has. And no one here is running. I didn't know H had another name? His full name is Holy Spirit?"

I don't speak. I answer his question with a nod, and he continues.

"It's different in here; it's a welcoming feeling. And those eyes aren't so scary. Then there's that pretty, smart teacher.

I was in a class before H, I mean Holy Spirit, pulled me out of there. They always worked in tandem or groups. They were called spirits also, but not holy. But seeing He is Holy and a Spirit, and the teacher welcomed Him as a special guest, and the way they locked eyes...."

I think, "I'm surprised Sir notices all this and comes to conclusions."

He just continues and says, "I'd wager a big sum on them being related. Do you know if that teacher is a spirit and works with or for Him?"

Sir's eyes shift towards Holy Spirit as he asks me this point-blank question. His comments cause me to think. He has been in other classrooms. This setting is not different for him, except it's a class with a different topic, a different spiritual atmosphere. By his comments about Wisdom, I can sense he's being drawn to her. I know Holy Spirit has this under control.

"Your will be done here, Papa. Your kingdom come into this place. Flood us all with Your overwhelming goodness. Amen."

With Sir still leaning towards me, I say to him, "You are making some great observations and asking some really good questions. Why don't we just listen up and see where we go from here. Listen to Holy Spirit. He may give us some insight."

Holy Spirit addresses the class and then looks to Wisdom. "Thank You for the invitation to come into the class today."

I see what Sir saw, the deep connection between the Spirit of Wisdom and Holy Spirit. Then it occurs to me, Holy Spirit is here. Wisdom is here . . .. They all must be here. I'm not sure if everyone sees what I see, but the manifestation and opening of the Spirit realm at the front of the classroom overshadows everything Wisdom manifested on the blackboard. The room is filled with an overwhelming feeling of Their presence. They all are here! Whoa.

I hear a rattle. Sir is leaning over to me again. "Man," he says, "the light got brighter in here, and it even feels better. Do you notice that?"

I'm amazed at how spiritually in tune he is. Then again, he did mention he was in class with spirits teaching. I know it can't be teaching like I would think of teaching. But either way, it was spiritual instruction or control of some sort.

In my pondering, I notice a separation happening. Wisdom moves to the side of the room, continuing to manifest as the female teaching us. Then, like vapors of light, the remaining Spirits of the Lord flow out of Holy Spirit around us in the room. The seven Spirits of the Lord are in a circle around us.

Sir is on it. He says, "Now, I can feel it. She is a Spirit and Holy Spirit has a team with Him. Are we in trouble? Will we be disciplined for something we didn't even know we did?"

I calm him down by saying, "We are not in trouble. All is good. You said it yourself, 'No one is running.' They are here to assist Holy Spirit, that's all."

Sir says, "He didn't need any assistance the first time I saw Him. He was in total control of the circumstances."

I think about his discernment. Sir is moving into suspicion and expecting some type of discipline.

Me, I'm moved from my classroom seat back to my living room chair. It's been a full day that started in my library chair, then to the job site, and back to my living room chair. My thoughts were focused on the classroom events as I went about my day. I have to believe I'll be brought back into the classroom for what's coming next.

"Thank you, Papa, for this amazing day You gave me. Thank You for interrupting it like You did. Help me to sleep well tonight. I give You this time to continue to speak to me through dreams. Amen."

SECOND STEP

While I'm sitting in my library chair praising and waiting on Him, a soft rain begins to fall. The continuous sound of the rain hitting the metal roof moves me into the spirit realm.

I wasn't expecting to see what I see. All is dark around me, and I see two yellow eyes constantly moving in quick, short movements to the left and to the right. Shadows appear, and I see the eyes are in the head of some type of bird. The head doesn't stop moving, and the bird seems anxious. It seems to be looking for something and looking out for something.

The room becomes brighter, although there are still shadows that hinder me from seeing everything in the room. I feel a ring of spirits around me, and I start to feel uneasy. I pray, "Papa, bring clarity. Where am I? What's happening here?"

Light slowly manifests around me. The ring of spirits around me becomes clearer. The ring is the manifestation of the seven Spirits of the Lord. "Please forgive me, Papa, for feeling uneasy." I feel His peace and reassurance. All is good.

The yellow eyes and the bird are still there. It's not a big bird, but in the darkness and only seeing the eyes, it seemed bigger. The eyes are out of proportion compared to the size of the bird. The claws of the bird are latched onto the link of a chain. Then the chain seems to move. I realize this is a chain across the left shoulder of Sir. My immediate response is to speak out and chase the bird off him. I feel restrained in my spirit by two hands on my shoulders and another covering my heart. I don't speak.

I pray internally in my spirit, "Please give me understanding, Papa.

What's happening here?"

I know Holy Spirit is in the front of the room. A female voice to my left softly whispers, "He's got this. Holy Spirit is causing the spirit of suspicion to rise up in Sir."

H says to me, "I am bringing you Understanding. Might is holding you still, and Knowledge is filling your heart with peace."

Understanding interjects, "Expect Sir to feel the overflow and slide his chair away, but Wisdom will pull him back."

As Understanding says this to me, chains rattle, and Sir slides his chair away. I see a different look on his face as suspicion tries to control him.

Wisdom speaks from across the room. She says, "In the presence of Holy Spirit, the atmosphere changes, and what was there has to leave."

Sir's attention is drawn to Her and the words She spoke. Her words cause him to slide back to me and ask, "What is happening here? I feel a spirit from the past that's causing me to rebel, but I'm drawn to the words of the teacher."

Understanding speaks into my spirit, "Sir is having spiritual flash backs brought on by the Holy presence manifesting in the room. Holy Spirit is using Us to bring this manifestation through the reverent Fear of the Lord. This is causing a mix of the old and the new, bringing up the past but drawing Sir to the new."

I ask, spirit to Spirit, "What am I to do?"

I hear, "Tell him, 'You are experiencing dimensional aspects of the spirit realm, nothing else.'"

I nod and say, "Sir, you are experiencing dimensional aspects of the spirit realm." I feel a hand on my mouth.

Understanding whispers, "You said all you need to say. Continue to pray." I feel prayer ramp up in my spirit.

She says, "This is Might causing you to pray in a powerful way spirit to Spirit. Keep it there, in the spirit. As you keep it there, you give Us access to work."

Sir nods his head and says, "I thought something like that was going on. Last time I was in a class with the spirits, I felt something added. Whatever they added caused me to not sleep at night and also caused me to think there was something around every corner. I'm feeling this again, but it's not as controlling."

Knowledge speaks into my spirit, "I am bringing a knowing to him, and Understanding will do her work. Keep praying."

I feel the intensity of this in my spirit and continue to pray. The hand on my mouth keeps my prayers in the spirit.

Sir looks at me and says, "I see it. There it is. What was imparted is sitting on my shoulder."

"Yes," Knowledge says into my spirit, "He is seeing the manifestation. This is good when it rises up and shows itself. Then it can be dealt with."

Wisdom speaks from across the room "Holy Spirit has some work to do. Let's bow our heads." I feel this is a cue to the students to pray. The holy atmosphere thickens in the room.

The yellow eyes of suspicion now dart back and forth rapidly. I see the spirit lean into Sir's head. Sir shakes his head and tries to pull away from the spirit. The spirit senses a pushback from him and backs out. Something larger now stands behind him. Two ugly claw-like hands are placed on his shoulders.

I am beginning to freak out.

Knowledge says into my spirit, "Peace, peace. Calm down. This is good. Suspicion called for the aid of control. Keep praying."

The chains rattling intensifies. Sir is being shaken by control, while suspicion has leaned back into his head. Even though they are working intensely on him, he is resisting. I pray James 4:7 and 8 in my spirit, *"Therefore, submit to God. Resist the devil and he will flee from you. Draw near to God and He will draw near to you."*

Praying those verses seems to give Sir strength to resist. Next, Holy Spirit begins to manifest in front of us. His eyes begin to burn like fire. This fire is focused in on Sir.

He speaks like thunder, "Come out and flee from this place."

Sir shakes violently. Suspicion flies off, and the hands of control are removed from his shoulders. I hear a loud rattling of chains and then a clunk.

All is quiet, and light fills the room.

Sir, who seemed to go unconscious, is shaking his head. I see a couple of chains laying on the floor next to him. The students also see them. Two jump up from their chairs and drag them to the door and pile them on top of his coat. The students hurry back to their seats.

Sir, regains consciousness, looks at me, and asks, "What just happened?"

The hand is released from my mouth, and I know this is permission to speak. I say, "Some old friends of yours have left, and you have been freed up to ask more of them to leave. Now you can welcome new friends into your life. New friends who won't try to control you."

At first Sir is at a loss for words. Then he says, "I feel different, like I can move a little better. Things feel lighter."

When he says "lighter," I see the circle around us recede back into Holy Spirit.

He says, "H, Holy Spirit, showed up in power, didn't He? He must have. I heard shrieks and thought I saw spirits running."

I respond with, "Yes, He did, and I believe I saw and heard what you did."

Sir nods and says to me, "Quite a class we are in, and that teacher looks prettier than when I first got here."

I look to Wisdom, and She nods and winks at me.

Holy Spirit is behind us as at the start. He leans over and whispers into my left ear, "Second step. We are making headway." I nod, smile, and look at Sir, who is smiling also.

The rain that brought me into the spirit realm now brings me back to my library chair. Thankfulness saturates my being like the spring rain soaking the ground.

I close my eyes and whisper a prayer of gratitude to Papa.

"Thank You for the process in Sir's life and in all our lives. Amen."

HOUSE CLEANING - IT'S A PROCESS

As I wake from another full night's restful sleep, I'm led to Luke 11:24–26. This section is titled, "An Unclean Spirit Returns" in my Bible.

"When an unclean spirit goes out of a man, he goes through dry places, seeking rest; and finding none, he says, 'I will return to my house from which I came.' And when he comes, he finds it swept and put in order. Then he goes and takes with him seven other spirits more wicked than himself, and they enter and dwell there; and the last state of that man is worse than the first."

This passage is also referenced in Matthew 12:43-45.

I think, "Is there a reason I'm led to this passage upon waking up?" I bless my spirit to be out front and speak to my natural mind, will, and emotions to line up behind my spirit. I pray, "Come, Holy Spirit, and bring revelation about this scripture in my mind this morning." His presence settles around me and my chair. I feel encapsulated in the love of His presence.

Through this love, I hear the voice of Wisdom speak, "You know this feeling. You have walked in the reality of not only feeling loved but feeling accepted. In Sir's case, he has not felt this in a long time. He has been more at home with the feelings of control and suspicion than with the love of the Father. Pray these scriptures over him. Continue to pray them as We continue to clean and sweep his house.

"You see, it's a process. One can clean up, but until the house is swept, there is a residue of dust. We are in the cleaning process, and things that have been settled in him have dust on them. When they are removed, the dust becomes unsettled and will settle in another place in the house. After the house is cleaned, swept, and put in order, it needs to be filled. As we sweep, clean, and bring order, We will grace his house with Our presence. When the spirits come back and see Our presence, they will see they have no access."

I begin to pray for Sir, "Father, I thank You for the cleaning process in Sir's life. I speak and impart strength to him, that he may feel Your presence and acceptance, that what has been familiar to him will be repulsive to him, that he will accept Your gift of freedom and let You fill his house with Your presence. I accept him as a brother. Lead me in how to continue to pray for him. I bless You in this process, and I bless him to receive from You through the power of Your Son, Jesus, who lives in me. Amen."

To my right I hear a chair move and something sliding. It sounds like steel being dragged over wood. I look toward the sound and see Sir leaning over to me. The sound is coming from the remaining chains scraping across the back of the wooden chair he sits in.

He says to me, "Hey, I never got your name? You knew who I was when we met, but all I know is you're a friend of Holy Spirit."

"This is good," I'm thinking, "He didn't call Holy Spirit 'H,' and he's asking my name." I respond with a smile and say, "People refer to me as Colonel."

"That's an interesting name, but I guess so is Sir. Very nice to make your acquaintance, Colonel," he says as he nods.

I ask, "How you feeling, Sir?"

He hesitates, then says, "Well, I'm sure I feel accepted by you and that little girl. I wonder what her name is. Do you know, Colonel?"

I shake my head, "No, but I imagine we will see her again, so we can ask."

Then Sir says, "I feel accepted by that pretty teacher also and the team Holy Spirit brought with Him. Do you know her name?"

I nod and tell Sir, "Her name is Wisdom."

"That's interesting," Sir says, "I always associated wisdom with an old person sitting in a comfortable chair or under a tree on a park bench. A person who is unapproachable, you know, you have to be invited to be in their presence, invited by them." He looks intently at me as he talks and continues, "But she seems very approachable and speaks words I can understand."

I nod. "Yes, I understand. I have felt the same way sometimes with wise, older people I have met."

"Anyway," he says, "I'm glad Holy Spirit came with you to get me and bring me here. What do you think the next lesson will be?"

"Well, that's up to Her," as I nod towards Wisdom, "I believe She, Holy Spirit, and the team have much more in store for us. For me, I'm on a long-term plan with Their lessons. It seems like each lesson naturally leads to another and builds on what the previous lesson taught."

"That's interesting," he says. "The other spirit classes I was in piled it in ya. Some days felt so heavy I couldn't walk. Then I would get used to the weight of that lesson and get another one piled on. But you're saying that we've had a lesson? And already I feel lighter. Must be these are different lessons."

"Yes," I respond. "There are different kinds of lessons. Although the topic is weighty, it's not a heavy burden to carry. It's almost like learning to unlearn. What I mean by that is it's like cleaning a room or a house. When you realize you have something you don't need anymore, you can get rid of it to make more room for the new. It's understanding what doesn't work for you anymore, and getting rid of it to make room for something new that does work. You get rid of the clutter and then sweep up the area."

I can tell I hit a cord with Sir. His fists clench like he's holding onto something. But I'm rescued by the little girl and a friend she has with her.

Sir's hands relax, and he smiles.

I look to Wisdom, nod, and say in my spirit, "Thank You."

She smiles and nods back and speaks to my spirit, "Good start. Keep praying." Her eyes go to the little girl and her friend, "They will take it from here." I start praying in the spirit and keep it there.

Sir says, "We were just talking about you," as he motions towards me.

I smile and nod.

She says in kind of a sassy tone, "Oh yeah, was it good?

"This little girl seems older than she looks," I think.

Sir says, "Why, yes. Why would it be anything but that? We were really wondering what your name is. You called me Mr. Sir, and that's nice, but what's your name, and who's your friend here?" pointing to the little boy.

She says, "My name is Shama."

"Please say that again," he says, "a little slower."

She says, "Sure. Sha-ma," as she nods her head for inflection.

He says, "Sha-ma."

She nods and says, "Yeah, that's it." Then she turns to her friend, a boy about her age with almost white-blond hair and fair skin. "This is Ollie," pointing her left thumb over her shoulder, "and he has a question for you, Mr. Sir."

Ollie steps up and puts his hand out to shake Mr. Sir's hand and says, "Hi, I'm Ollie."

Sir hesitates and looks at me.

I say, "He won't bite you. He is greeting you like a man. It's okay to shake his hand."

Sir slowly brings his hand up from his lap and takes Ollie's hand and shakes it. Pulling his hand back after the shake, he looks at it and says to me, "That was nice. Maybe need to do that more often."

I nod and don't say a word. It's their time to talk to Sir, not mine.

Sir leans a little forward and says, "What's your question, young fella?" Ollie hesitates and lowers his head.

Shama hits him on the shoulder and says, "Go ahead. He's not going to bite ya." She smiles and looks at me.

Ollie says, "I was wondering, uh. You see, I'm making this, well, I got a piece of wood. It's a real nice piece of wood I found out back."

Shama hits him again on the shoulder.

He says to her, "Quit that. I'm gettin' there."

Sir doesn't say anything. He is amused as he watches intently.

Ollie continues, "I want to make a swing with the piece of wood and that little chain there around your chest," as he points to a thin chain. "Would be good to hang the swing on. If you would like to let me borrow it, I can bring it back."

Sir sits up straight with a jerk in his chair and crosses his arms, covering the chain Ollie pointed at.

Sir's lips are tight as a clam shell. I pray more intensely for Sir to give it up. He doesn't look at Ollie, but his head moves very slowly left and right, signaling a no. He looks at me and says, "This young man is pretty bold. He doesn't know about this award."

I say, "Well, you want to tell him?"

Shama says, "I'd like to hear about your award," and hits Ollie's shoulder.

He says, "Ouch!" rubbing his shoulder while he looks at Shama. She motions with her head at Sir.

Ollie says, "Oh yeah, me too. I'd like to hear about your award too."

Shama jumps up in the chair next to Sir where she sat before and says to Ollie, "Get a chair so we can listen to Mr. Sir."

Ollie quickly drags a chair over, scraping it across the floor. I look past Ollie and see Wisdom glowing and the other Spirits of the Lord starting to manifest. I increase my prayer in the spirit.

Sir loosens his arms and leans a little forward. He turns to me and says, "I've not told anyone about my rewards before. They always told me the rewards were mine and were internal. This chain Ollie wants is woven through all of them. Kind of holds everything together."

I realize he used the word *reward* twice, not *award*. It's amazing how things can be twisted and interwoven. I feel to tell him, "You don't need to get into the nitty gritty about the rewards. Just hit the highlights. They will catch on and ask questions if they don't understand."

The Spirit of Understanding stands behind me, leans over, and speaks into my spirit, "I'm here to direct the understanding of his rewards."

Nodding to her, I also direct my nod to Sir and say, "Go ahead. This may be good for you to explain."

At this point, I need to pause and move on with my day in the natural. I know I'll be brought back to this place with Sir, Shama, and Ollie.

"Please seal this time, Papa. Then bring me back in Your timing. Amen."

THE UNRAVELING

Sitting in His presence this morning on the lanai, I feel a slight breeze blowing over me. This is not a typical breeze of His Spirit. The breeze starts at my feet and covers my body from the ground up.

"Thank You, Papa, for coming today in the breeze. My spirit is out front to receive from You. I thank You that Holy Spirit is with You here. Where do You want to take me today?"

The breeze lifts me up and moves me back to the classroom with Sir, Shama, and Ollie. Understanding is close behind us. The figure of a woman representing Wisdom manifests in front of the class. I see another of the seven Spirits standing beside Ollie's chair. Shama sees this Spirit also, looks at me, and says, "Mr. Sir," turning towards him, "I believe Counsel is here today, and when you tell us about your rewards, we can all talk about it, with your permission of course."

I'm amazed at the wisdom flowing through this little girl.

I hear Understanding in my spirit, "She is speaking, being guided by Wisdom through Might."

As Understanding says "Might," I see another of the seven Spirits behind Shama. I have to believe this is Might speaking through her. I'm amazed again at how all this is coming together in the spirit within the spiritual realm where we are.

I hear, "You are in multiple dimensions of the spiritual realm."

I thank Understanding for giving understanding. I lean over to Sir and say, while nodding to Ollie and Shama, "You have a captive audience here. How are you going to tell us about your rewards?"

He leans slightly forward and says while looking at Ollie, "I wasn't too much older than you, young fella. My life was filled with fun and activities, playing outside with my friends. But I wanted to be in charge. This meant I wanted to be in control and tell them what to do. I started making up stories about each of them that weren't true."

I feel a need to ask a question but a hand slips over my mouth. I say to Understanding in the spirit, "I understand."

Ollie and Shama don't move, but they look at me. I realize they hear my thoughts in the spirit.

Shama says to me in the spirit, "Wisdom is guiding us. We got this through Counsel and Might. Wisdom's words are directed to me, but I know they hear them also." Then she says to me, "Continue to pray in the spirit. This will give them an openness to hear Us and allow Sir to release what holds him captive."

Shama and Ollie both nod their heads as part of the Spirit-to-spirit conversation. It is awesome how the communication through the spirit realm works.

I pray in my spirit with an intensity I haven't felt before. Through this prayer, I see what looks like a ring of fire around us, even encompassing the seven Spirits.

Understanding says, "Ring of angels sent by the Father. He is providing covering; your intercession is being heard and activated. Continue in the spirit."

I nod and continue in the spirit. My intercession intensifies. Looking at Ollie and Shama, I see their eyes focus in on Sir.

Shama says, "Oh, Mr. Sir, did you lose your friends by telling untrue stories?"

He responds, "At first some started to separate themselves from me, but then one by one they started to believe the stories about each other and started doing what I made up in the stories. That was when I noticed my first reward. In the spirit class I was taken to I was given this little chain that you pointed to, Ollie."

Ollie's eyebrows lift, and he asks, "Where was this class you were taken to?"

Sir says, "That's a good question, young fella. I guess I'm getting ahead of myself. I didn't think much of the class at first because it was a dream I had. But after a while, the dreams got more involved, even to the point I didn't want to go to sleep. But that didn't happen at first. So, backing up," Sir puts his right hand on his chin as he thinks. He mutters, "Sometimes it's hard to think. It's like my mind is cloudy."

"Pray into that," I hear in my spirit, "It's manifesting. It's showing itself."

I focus my prayers in the spirit on the cloudiness of his mind. I see a cloud around his mind. I know Ollie and Shama see it, also.

Shama says, "Your friend Holy Spirit is my friend also." This causes Sir to turn and look directly at her. Shama takes that as a cue and says, "I ask my friend and your friend Holy Spirit to come and blow the cloudy fog away. Is it okay that we ask Him to do that for you? To clear your mind so you can continue to tell us about your rewards?"

Sir nods and says, "Let's give that a try."

With his permission, Shama sits up straighter in her seat and says in a sweet voice, "Holy Spirit, You are our friend. Come with a gentle breeze and blow away the cloud of this fog around Mr. Sir's mind."

I feel a whoosh of wind, and the air is cleared.

Shama says to Sir, "How's that, Mr. Sir? Better?"

Sir shakes his head and says, "Yes, that's much better. Things are even clearer here in this room."

Ollie says, "Good. Now can you tell us about the dream and the reward?" pointing to the chain.

Sir says, "Yes, the reward. I later learned that this reward had a kind of unseen power, and I liked the power it gave me. It was power over people without being in control of them. I could just say things that made them do what I wanted them to do. Being young I didn't know what the name was for the reward but learned later it was called manipulation."

Understanding taps me on the shoulder, "There it is. Pray for an unraveling of manipulation." I focus in on it in the spirit.

I hear Sir start to cough, and his hands go to his chest.

Ollie, guided by Counsel through Wisdom says, "We are here to help you unweave that chain."

Sir's words are gasps, like he can't breathe.

Ollie says in a commanding voice, which surprises me based on how he first spoke to Sir, "Mr. Sir, your friend Holy Spirit is here. Let Him go deep to when and where this chain is attached and pull that manipulation out of you. You don't need that anymore. It's only holding you back from who you are."

Ollie doesn't even ask. He commands, "Come, wind of Holy Spirit, come and fill Mr. Sir's lungs so he can breathe. And with the breath of Your Spirit, reach in and grab this chain at the root and pull it out."

Sir's eyes get big, and he gasps out another few words, "Can this be? If so, come Holy Spirit."

I see the Spirit hand of Holy Spirit reach into Sir and grab the inner end of the small chain. As Holy Spirit starts to pull the chain, Sir starts to shake and then spin in his chair. Holy Spirit is pulling the string on a top. I hear a rattling and clanging and sliding of chain on chain. Then a shriek. Sir cries out, "Mercy! Give me Mercy!"

I look at Shama. She is interceding also. I sense the power of her prayers through Might as Sir is being set free from this intertwined chain of manipulation in his life.

Whoa, this is not pretty, but it's beautiful to see him being set free.

I hear more clunking on the floor as more chains fall off. Understanding gives me intel through the spirit, and I pray specifically. The chain Holy Spirit is pulling releases a chain of lying and a chain of hypnotism. They fall to the ground as I see dark images flee the room.

Other students run and grab the chains and pile them on top of the pile by the door. Sir stops spinning and sits straighter in his chair as the end of the chain comes off and out of him. A few more clunks on the floor.

In the midst of this two-hour session, I feel the need to pause.

"Is this okay, Papa? "

He says, "We are here and will be here."

I feel His release to pause.

FREEDOM'S REALITY

The days have been full with our volunteer work at Youth With A Mission (YWAM) Ships in Hawaii. The spiritual activity is high as the students wind down on the lecture phase and get ready for outreach. My time in the spirit has also been full.

I pray, "Thank You, Papa, for showing me what You've been showing me. Thank You for letting me partner with all of this. My spirit man is out front this morning, waiting on You. I bless my ears to hear and my eyes to see what You have for me today. Please send Holy Spirit to lead and guide me today in all I do. Amen."

The peaceful cooing of a dove draws me into the spirit realm. I find myself right back where we paused yesterday. A pile of chains lay on the floor around Sir's chair. Sir's chains were loosened, and he was released from demonic influence when Holy Spirit brought a whirlwind of deliverance.

Again, students jump up to remove the chains, dragging them to the pile. Looking at Sir, I see a handsome man who was buried under all the weight of the chains of bondage. I see new brightness in his countenance.

I feel another presence behind me. I sense another of the seven Spirits of the Lord has intel for us.

I hear, "Yes, I do."

I recognize that voice as the voice of Knowledge. I see Shama and Ollie recognize His voice also. These two have been taught well, and their perception in the Spirit realm is exceptional.

He says, "Sir is almost free. There are two more strongholds in his life. He thought manipulation was the first, but the others came in before that. The two remaining are shame and pride. Shame came in when he was abused by his step uncle, causing him to be a loner as a child. He didn't have a grid for what happened to him.

"This gave way for pride to move in and tell him he was special. Pride convinced him he was better than others because he survived what happened. Pride has been running the show, so to speak, and is strong in his life. Pride will even use shame to control him, as you will see.

"Be prepared, Colonel. You know your position. You pray into these things, and you will have backup from the other students in the class. As Shama and Ollie are led by Counsel and Wisdom, your prayers will continue to give Us all power to work through them. Understanding will give the nudge when it is time to speak. Expect Might to speak through your words. Greater are We in you three than those who are controlling him and in him."

I realize Knowledge has been speaking to all of us in the spirit, giving us all assignments and confirming what we have been doing. It's almost like we are on a secure channel so the spirits controlling Sir don't hear.

Sir looks like he feels good about what has happened. I begin to pray in the spirit, moving into intercession with my spirit man out front. In the spirit I can hear the prayers of the students join in as I'm praying. I even sense a heightened angelic presence and activity in the room.

Shama is the first one to speak. "How you feeling, Mr. Sir?" she asks. It's quiet, almost to the point of awkwardness, but she waits.

I see Ollie is waiting and listening for Understanding to lead him. The patience of the two is wonderful to watch. They are not anxious as they wait.

Sir finally speaks, "I feel good, but I feel that I'm taking up too much of your time. It seems like I'm the center of attention, and I probably need to be by myself."

I see Wisdom intently looking at Shama. I know she is receiving from Her.

"Not so, Mr. Sir," Shama says to him. We are here with you and for you. At times I have felt like what you described and even felt like I was abandoned or orphaned. But the Teacher, as she points to Her with her right thumb without taking her eyes off Sir, tells us in those times when we are close to getting all Holy Spirit has for us, we need to stay connected."

The spirit of pride rises up in Sir and speaks through him, "I am connected, and my connection is strong. I don't need little kids telling me what to do."

I feel like getting in his face for saying that and realize the spirit of pride is trying to get on us through Sir. Ollie and Shama are at total peace.

Ollie speaks up and says, "Yeah, sometimes we don't think we need adults telling us what to do either. But we aren't telling you anything. You have told us you have been in spirit classes before, and you feel this class is a spirit class. So why do you think it's us telling you what to do?"

Sir is lost for words. Ollie is at total peace. Me? I'm amazed at what came from him but know it's Counsel and Might working through him.

I feel a shift as we continue to intensify our prayers.

Sir says, "Maybe so, but I'm not worthy of all this attention. You are all nice, but are you really interested in my rewards?" Even in the freedom Sir has gained, his mind is still being controlled by pride working through shame.

I hear in my spirit, "Zero in on this in prayer. This is the stronghold."

I focus my prayer. "Father, you have given us authority through Jesus. Using that authority, I ask through Wisdom that You would give me the words to pray." I feel a swelling in my spirit and a hand on my mouth as I pray in the spirit against the two remaining spirits controlling Sir.

I see my prayers in action as Shama jumps off her chair. She does it so quickly Sir jumps in his seat. Ollie stands up at this point also, and the two of them are now standing in front of Sir.

He says to them, "Oh, are you leaving me to myself? Why would you leave me at a time like this?"

I think, "Wow, that shame is really messing with his mind."

Understanding says, "You're seeing it and hearing it. Pray into it. The spirit is manifesting. It's showing itself and can be cast out."

I pray.

Shama looks right at him and says, "We see you, spirit of shame. You have messed with this man's mind long enough, and it's time for you to go. By the authority we have through Jesus, we stand in agreement and tell you to leave this man! Go!"

I feel the power of her words as she and Ollie stand in agreement, casting this spirit out. Another chain falls to the floor. A dark slithering cloud gusts up quickly and is blown away by the wind of Holy Spirit.

Sir straightens up in his chair, making himself look really big in front of the two of them. Pride speaks through him and says, "You will never get me to leave him. He's mine and has been mine since he was young."

Ollie takes a step towards Sir, looks directly into his eyes, and says in a peaceful tone, "You're wrong. He's not yours. His life has been paid for by the blood of Jesus."

When Ollie says "Jesus," Sir's hands go over his ears, and pride shrieks.

With his voice still calm, Ollie says, "Pride, your time is up. I command you to come out of him and go to the dry places to be crushed under the feet of Jesus."

The last chain falls to the floor. Sir slumps in his chair. A dark thick cloud comes out of him, shrieking. Students run to drag the chains of shame and pride to the pile.

I see Holy Spirit behind Shama and Ollie. He walks right through them and picks Sir up to embraces him. Looking over Sir's shoulder, Holy Spirit's eyes of fire burn up the pile of chains at the door. A student runs with a broom. Another runs and opens the door, and the ashes of the burned-up chains are swept out the door. Then the door is closed.

Still in the embrace of Holy Spirit, Sir is sobbing. He says, "Yes, I believe. Jesus has set me free. Fill me with His love." I see Holy Spirit manifest into the figure of Jesus as Sir is being filled with the love of Jesus. The seven Spirits of the Lord come around Sir, who is being embraced by Jesus, and flow into Jesus as He's embracing Sir.

I hear in my spirit "Cleaned, swept, set in order, and filled. Now the seal is being set by the seven Spirits of the Lord."

A soft breeze blows over me. Shama and Ollie wink. I give them a thumbs up, and I'm moved to the sunshine and my chair on the lanai.

My natural mind is reeling at what just happened. The free and filled appearance of Sir embedded in my mind and spirit is the reality of a life set free in Jesus.

"Thank You, Papa, for letting me be in this class. Help me walk in more of the reality of Your freedom today. Amen."

YOU, YOUR SPIRIT

Sitting in the chair on the lanai this morning, I'm immediately moved into the spirit realm. The figure of a man walks directly towards me. He is a flaming fire and walks with a consistent, methodical cadence. As he gets closer to me, his size increases.

He doesn't stop! I am lifted to a standing position, and the man of fire walks into me.

I don't shake. I feel no heat. I feel the same but know something has happened to me. Next, the figure of the man walks out of me. Same methodical cadence as he walks away from me, except he's not on fire. The man walking away from me is black like charcoal, like something that was on fire, but is not burning now. He continues to walk and then disappears.

Then everything in front of me starts to rapidly move away. To my left, to my right, in front of me, everything is expanding and moving. Again, I see the man of fire walking towards me with the same pace and cadence. Again, he walks directly into me and then out of me, looking like charcoal.

Everything that was expanding from me is now coming back into me. There is still no feeling in my natural body, but I feel totally different in my spirit.

I look down and see my body glowing like metal glows after it's been heated in fire. Out of my chest appears a hook made of hot, glowing metal. Then another hot, glowing hook appears, coming down in front of me. It looks similar to the hook coming out of my chest. The second hook connects to the hook coming out of me and begins to lift me up rapidly. What appears to be hot, glowing, connected metal gets brighter and looks hotter as I am pulled by the hook that's hooked to me.

The heat from these hooks is transferred into my body, and my whole body looks like the molten, glowing metal of the hooks. I can see into it. I see it moving within itself as it glows.

I look straight ahead. In the distance I see a blue body of water. I am moving fast and get closer to it. The water appears to be crystal clear and is also moving within itself. It's not a churning or a bubbling, but it's a depth that appears to look alive.

Then I'm plunged into this water. I hear the sizzling sound of hot metal as it's submerged into water to be cooled and tempered. The hook holding me is released, and the hook in my chest retracts back into me.

I'm now submerged in the water. Everything is blue like the color of the sky, and everything is alive. The water continues to move. I feel as if I'm one with the water around me. In this state of oneness I ask, "Papa, what is happening? The man of fire, the molten hooks, the body of water, the oneness?"

Then I am picked up like a baby from a bath with two hands holding me. Water drips off me, and a warm breeze begins to blow over my being. After I'm totally dry, I'm placed back into my chair on the lanai. The empty chair next to me begins to glow and fills with a vaporous cloud of a person. I know this is Holy Spirit manifesting next to me. My body starts to tremble from His presence being so close.

Without leaving the chair, the presence expands and fills the space around me. It feels like I'm back in the water, but this is a moving, vaporous presence around me. A holy fear comes over me as the vapor seems to divide into seven but somehow remains as one. I realize these are the seven Spirits of the Lord manifesting out of Holy Spirit. There is nowhere for me to go except in. I'm enveloped into the vaporous cloud. Everything around this cloud I'm in seems to get darker. Not totally black, just darker, like it's overshadowed by the vapor cloud.

Out of the cloud, I hear the voice of Understanding. The voice says, "The Man of Fire, Jesus, has walked into you this morning. Not you, your body, but you, your spirit. He did this twice as a witness to you. He confirmed within Himself that He has placed into your spirit His all-consuming fire. It's a Spirit fire that manifests through your spirit, not your body. This is why you didn't tremble in your body. Your body stayed in the chair this morning, and we took your spirit man on a short journey.

"The molten hook of fire coming out of you was your spirit, and it was hooked to His fire. His fire without melded with His fire within to engulf you. Your spirit man was totally in Him. Next, your spirit on fire connected to His fire and carried you to the lake of His presence. The moving water is His presence within the water. When submerged into the lake of His presence, your spirit on fire was tempered by the lake of His presence. The fire of His life in your spirit and the water from the lake of His presence around you, your spirit, in Him. He has galvanized you, your spirit, in Himself. He, the All in all, in all. Holy Spirit then carried you, your spirit, back. He dried the spirit, you, with His own warm breath and placed your tempered spirit back into you, your body."

The voice of Understanding now defers to the voice of Wisdom, "Things will be different from a spiritual perspective. There will be an enhanced clarity of the scriptures. There will be a flow of His Spirit off the pages into your spirit. There will be a flow of Us, His Spirit, through holy fear through you, your spirit, to others, to their spirits.

"The connections will be like the molten hooks connecting your spirits to His. You, your natural mind, will not be able to figure this out or work this out. This is Spirit to spirit, His to yours, through the holy fear of Him to manifest Him."

Wisdom turns and nods to Knowledge who says, "Knowing will come through Us through His holy fear when you, your spirit, needs to know. Like Wisdom said, 'this is Spirit to spirit, His to yours.' That's all you, your spirit, needs to know right now. I will manifest when needed."

Knowledge turns to Counsel who says, "Through Them, pointing to Understanding, Wisdom, and Knowledge, I will be there to guide your spirit to speak or listen. Might will bring power."

I see the Spirit of Might leaning on an invisible wall, arms crossed, nodding His head.

Understanding says, "Your natural mind has been bypassed. Your spirit has drawn this in, and it will be drawn out by Him in His timing and placement."

Wisdom interjects, "Timing and placement are His. Connection is His. Expect deeper spiritual connections as We connect you, and as your spirit connects to who He has for you, your spirit, to connect to."

A hush comes from Them, and the vaporous cloud is absorbed back into His presence in the chair next to me. Then the chair is empty. I ask myself the question, "Or is it empty?" I know in the natural it is, but in the spiritual that's a different question. A smile crosses my face as I, my natural self, am once again blown away by Their ever-so-close presence.

"Thank You, Papa, for the light of Your presence that has appeared to me this morning even before the natural sun has risen. I bless You today. Help me to be a blessing to those around me today. Amen."

BACK TO THE CLASSROOM

Sitting in my chair this morning on the lanai, I'm moved into the spirit realm. Everything in the spiritual realm in front of me is slowly drifting from my right to my left. I'm in a cloud. The cloud is moving around me, and I'm moving with it.

I hear Holy Spirit's voice within the cloud. "We are heading back to the classroom to checkup on Sir."

My heart is filled with excitement to see Sir again. I have been wondering how he is doing. I know Holy Spirit is not going there because He doesn't know how Sir is doing. He is taking me there to let me see how Sir is doing.

It seems like forever, and it seems like just minutes, when, suddenly, we are at the classroom door. I hear the voice of Understanding, "When you are in Their presence, you are in eternity with Them. Life as you know it in the natural doesn't exist. Your spirit is forever with Them in Their presence. You have always been and always will be. When you accepted Jesus into your heart, the reality of being with Them in eternity in the present opened to you. When you started to take notice of it in the spirit, it became real in the natural. It's the everything in nothing, and the nothing in everything you experienced in the spirit on your way to the classroom with Holy Spirit."

I think, "Wow! Understanding not only has a way with words but also a way of making me feel and understand them."

Knowledge speaks up and says, "Yes, she does. When people go to Understanding and Wisdom first, My part is easy. Too many people want to know something before they get understanding. Just having knowledge about a topic doesn't mean you know the topic. True spiritual understanding and wisdom through the fear of the Lord bring the heavenly perspective. Worldly or natural understanding and wisdom don't have this."

My mind is reeling with another "Wow!" and we are still outside the classroom. The overflow already coming from inside impacts my spirit man. Moving inside through the door, I see a burn mark on the floor by the door. This mark is the reminder of the chains being burned up after they came off Sir.

Knowledge says, "Those burn marks will continue to fade as Sir grows stronger in his understanding of what he is learning from Wisdom and Counsel."

I nod in thanks to Knowledge while we pass through the door. I see the Spirits of Wisdom and Counsel in front of the class. All the chairs are in a semi-circle. I know they have been having a virtual lesson on the blackboard. At first, I don't see Sir in the chairs, but then I spot him in a chair between Shama and Ollie.

Wisdom sees us come through the door and nods to Holy Spirit. Understanding and Knowledge take positions on the right and left of Holy Spirit. I naturally fall in behind them. I know I'm here to observe. For me these are some of the greatest lessons. So much is imparted to me as I observe how They interact with each other and those to whom They are imparting.

They move to just behind the semi-circle of chairs. I move to the side of the classroom, leaning against the wall to watch. Funny, when I lean against the wall, I lean into something otherworldly. I realize it's Might who's on standby.

I'm a little startled when He says, "Hi, Colonel. Great to see you here today."

I jump and say, "I didn't see You there."

He chuckles, "I know." Nodding at Sir, He says, "Sir is making great progress. One thing's for sure; in the spiritual classes of the evil one, he learned well how to learn. He is drawn into every word of Wisdom and Counsel. He will make a wonderful team leader when this group is sent into the warfare realm."

I respond, "Team leader? He is new to the group, and he is going to be the team leader?"

"Not Our call," as He nods towards Holy Spirit. "His call. He knows what He's doing, been at this a long time. Holy Spirit will move into different realms to pull those out who are the best fits for the Father's plan in another realm.

"Get them set free and train them in the things the Father has for them. Sir was not brought here from the warfare realm. He was brought here from the realm of confusion. He understands how that realm works and will work with his team against whomever the evil one sends into the warfare realm. Sir has the experience needed to overcome in that realm and lead this team to overcome in their mission there.

"The big thing Wisdom and Counsel are working on with Sir is the ability to defer to Us as he moves into that realm. You have some understanding about the weapons needed for this realm. The weapons are in the inside. Battles are fought and won in the warfare realm as Holy Spirit leads the natural spirit in each person. You worked with Us in this process when We walked Sir through his deliverance. We all function in this together with mankind.

"Isaiah 11:1-5 refers to the Rod, the Branch, and Him. All three of these are Jesus. When Jesus inhabits and rests in the heart of an individual, the Fear of the Lord will be his delight. Then the words of his mouth and his breath will slay the wicked with righteousness and justice. Righteousness and faithfulness will be the belt of his waist and loins. Father, Son, and Holy Spirit work through a submitted vessel, or group of vessels. Unity with Them uses Us to slay the wicked and establish His kingdom in that realm. This will extend to His kingdom being established in the earth, as it is in heaven."

I respond with, "Wow, I can tell all of You work together. For a moment there, I felt as if Understanding was speaking through You."

He responds, "Yes, We all are of the same Spirit, the Spirit of the Lord. When the Spirit of the Lord is upon you, the Fear of the Lord works through you. It activates Us to work in the spirit realm around and through you. Soon it will be totally natural for the eyes to see and the ears to hear in the spirit naturally."

Again, my mind is spinning, but I know my spirit is soaking all this in. This side-bar lesson from the Spirit of Might has taken me to another level of understanding.

A rush of wind next to me almost knocks me over. If it weren't for Might grabbing me, Holy Spirit would have knocked me over with His presence.

He says to me, "Yes, the whole class is moving into the next level. Even the seven Spirits are showing you the power of the flow They have between each other. They can defer to each other while representing Their own identity. This is possible because They are representing the identity of the Father."

He turns to look at the class, then towards Wisdom and Counsel, who nod back at Him. He nods at them, and I see Shama and Ollie smile and nod to each other. I know they feel Their presence in the room. Me? I get the overflow for being here. I think of a message I heard a while back. All we need to do is show up, and God will show off.

Holy Spirit leans into me and speaks into my spirit, "Sir is doing great. It won't be long now, and We will be sending them," as He waves over the class, "into the warfare realm. As We are assisting them on their important mission, these seats will be filled with another group. We will be teaching them, too. And this is only one classroom. Yes, to answer the question in your mind. There are more classrooms, with more students being trained and prepared for their respective missions in different realms."

I'm seeing a small glimpse of the vastness of the Father's master plan. Again, I hear in my spirit, "Yes, you are, and you have no idea of the vastness."

Everything starts to drift again around me. This time, from my left to my right. The classroom fades, and the sounds of natural life around the lanai replace that of the spiritual. I'm back with yet another valuable eternal lesson.

"Thank You, Papa, for this extended day of Spirit-led learning. Please impart it so deep in my spirit that it naturally becomes part of me. Amen."

SPIRIT DRIFT

In the time between sleep and awake a soft, female voice whispers in the ear of my spirit, "The more you spend time in His presence, the more you are changed."

My eyes pop open. I don't see anything in the room, but I feel a sweet presence.

I know I'm not dreaming. I'm not in a visitation. This is a voice in the spirit I hear as a wakeup call. Before long I'm up and out on the lanai in my chair.

I pray, "I position myself to hear more from You, Papa. I bless my spirit man to be out front. I speak to my natural mind, will, and emotions to come into alignment behind my spirit man. Amen.

"What else do You want to speak to me this morning Papa? Speak. Your servant is listening."

I close my eyes and wait on Him. I feel my spirit begin to drift. In front of me in the spirit, I see the infinity sign. Behind the infinity sign is a times sign. Behind that, another infinity sign.

I hear the female voice again, "The more you spend time in His presence, the more He moves you into the eternal. Infinity times infinity. There is no end to His presence, or to where He is taking you in His presence."

As I continue in this spirit drift, the female voice silences.

Next, I hear the rumble of another voice in the distance. This rumble causes my body to tremble. Tremble in a good way. I feel an overwhelming power flowing from the rumbling voice. The rumbling gets louder, and I feel wave after wave flowing into my spirit as I drift towards the rumble. I am moving in slow motion, and the atmosphere around me seems to be moving fast.

On my right, the atmosphere moves away from the rumble. On my left, it moves towards the rumbling voice. There is a sending and a calling happening simultaneously, and I'm in the middle of the sending and the calling. It's not a state of confusion. It's like the state between asleep and awake. Everything is moving, and I'm right in the middle of it.

The female voice speaks again, "You are in the middle of His presence. His presence causes some things to be repelled, and, at the same time, His presence causes other things to be attracted. Being in the middle allows you to see this atmospheric reality.

"The rumbling voice is His voice speaking who He is into the atmosphere. At His voice, the atmosphere changes. That's why you are changed in His presence. Nothing stays the same in His presence. Change is imminent. In the drift you have been being changed, and you are being changed. The heightened sensitivity of your spirit causes you to feel the drift, and the drift causes your spirit to become sensitive."

I feel the rumble of His voice again in my spirit. The words are, "I Am who I Am."

I'm reminded of how He answered Moses, when Moses asked Him, "Who shall I say you are?"

Then Moses said to God, "Indeed, when I come to the children of Israel and say to them, 'The God of your fathers has sent me to you,' and they say to me, 'What is His name?' what shall I say to them?"

And God said to Moses, "I AM WHO I AM." And He said, "Thus you shall say to the children of Israel, 'I AM has sent me to you.' " (Ex. 3:13-14)

The power of His voice must have shaken Moses to the core.

At His words I feel my spirit man shift in the drift. I'm picked up to a higher level while still in the middle of everything moving around me.

The female voice says again, "There are different levels in the shift of the drift. You feel like you are only drifting, but you are actually moving at eternal speed while in His presence. Being in the middle of His presence is being in the middle of eternity with Him. He has caused you to drift into this. All I did was make you aware of it. Yes, I am Wisdom and have been in His eternal presence from eternity."

Continuing, She says, "To answer the question in your mind, being in the middle of eternity is being in and with Him at any time on the spectrum of your time. He has no timeline, so whenever you are in His presence, you are in the middle of everything in Him. Wherever He is manifesting or making Himself known, that is the middle or the epicenter of everything.

"And, yes, to answer your other question, this is available for all who seek Him. There is plenty of room for all who desire to be in this place with Him. The problem is too many have not taken time to be still, as it says in Psalms 46:10.

Be still, and know that I am God;
I will be exalted among the nations,
I will be exalted in the earth!

"Being still doesn't mean not moving. It means quieting your mind until it is still. So still that nothing but Him is occupying or moving in it. This is a practiced discipline leading to the drift into His presence. When this discipline is learned, you don't realize you're going to quiet your mind. You just close your eyes, and everything but Him is stilled in your mind. It becomes natural, and His presence is the reality of all you are, because you're letting Him be All in all in you.

"This is not a matter of oneness with things around you in the natural. This is a oneness with the One who created you and all the natural surroundings around you. He is not the god of the tree, the rock, the water, the air, or the sky. Or whatever else has been worshiped. This is a oneness with the One who created all the things that have been worshiped. In this oneness all else pales in comparison."

The voice of Wisdom stops, and the rumble of His voice rolls back into Himself, where it came from. All is peaceful and quiet. The drift ceases, and I find myself back in my chair. I'm pondering all this, but the reality is much deeper than pondering. I will be in deep thought about this today.

Reviewing this visitation today, I see that Papa has taken me on a road trip He initiated through Wisdom just as I awakened today.

"Wow! What a God we serve! Thank You. Papa. I bless You and give You glory. Amen."

ETERNITY HAS BEGUN

It's early when I wake, but I know it's time to get up. While still in bed, I give thanks for a new day, "Thank You, Papa, for this day and a good night's sleep. I bless You today. Like the song lyrics say, 'Come rest on me. Come, Holy Spirit, and rest on me.'"

Holy Spirit quickly comes and fills the room with His presence.

With His presence, the spirit realm opens to me. In front of me I see two sides of a buckle. They are a dull yellow and appear to be made from plastic. Each side of the buckle is flat and has a tab sticking out of half of it. The two sides come together and insert into each other. There is a click, and the two sides appear as one. There doesn't seem to be any method of pulling the two sides apart, no lever to pull or button to push. If I hadn't seen them come together, I wouldn't realize they were two made into one. Focusing on the thing I'm calling a buckle, I don't see a strap coming from either side. It's only the buckle. Nothing else.

I quickly get up and head to my chair out on the lanai. His presence goes with me. After calling and blessing my spirit man to the front, I see a white, gloved right hand holding a small stick. The hand and stick are pointing down. Off to my right, in my peripheral vision, the shape of a man dressed in white appears. I look to my right, and in the natural I see only darkness. This must be part of the spiritual vision expanding to the side.

I focus on the white, gloved hand. I hear several clicks like I heard when the buckle-looking parts were brought together. I look at the stick being held by the hand, and my eyes follow it towards the direction it is pointed. A black and white checkered flag is attached to the stick.

Putting all this together in the mind of my spirit, I ask, "Papa, is there a race about to start? The buckles are clicked, and the white, gloved hand is holding a checkered flag. Is the man in white Jesus?"

I don't hear any words, and I don't see any people. All I see is the gloved hand holding the flag and several buckles floating in the air in front of me.

Then the man in white begins to walk towards the gloved hand holding the flag. As He gets closer, His presence starts to glow and shine. As He walks, He passes through the buckles. He passes each buckle, and a person appears with the buckle attached to a strap around each person. Each person is in a sitting position, floating in the air. There are hundreds and hundreds of people, maybe more. The people are men and women, children and adults, of all different nationalities. It's hard to estimate the number of people in front of me.

The man in white is Jesus, and He's walking towards me. My anticipation rises in my spirit about connecting with Him. My body begins to tremble as my spirit feels energy flowing from Him into me. He doesn't stop. He walks right through me. Total and complete fulfillment impact my spirit. My body moves with my spirit as it's impacted by His presence walking through me. After a slight pause in His walk, He is still for a moment. I am pulsating in the reality of His presence in me.

I hear a clicking and feel a slight pressure around my waist. I look down to see a right and left hand coming together around me. The fingers interlock and turn into the buckle. The arms the hands are attached to become the straps I see around the other people.

Looking up to Jesus, I see eyes with an eternal depth looking directly into mine. I begin to melt in His presence. I realize I'm looking into eternity in Him. He nods, and composure comes back into my being. Then He continues on His walk.

As my eyes follow Him, I see more and more people appear in front of me, floating in a sitting position, with the buckle and straps around them. Jesus walks to the gloved hand holding the flag and slides His hand into the glove. He stands in front of the countless number of people sitting in midair, strapped into invisible seats. It seems we are all ready for Him to raise the flag.

I hear a loud voice echoing around and above me, speaking this phrase, "Eternity has begun, and there are still more to come."

I think, "Eternity has begun. He is here. He is eternal. Who is still to come?"

Again, I hear, "Eternity has begun, and there are still more to come."

I feel another Presence next to me. A peaceful voice begins to speak. I know this voice. It's Holy Spirit. He puts me in total peace. "Eternity is Jesus the Son. Because He is here and He is eternal, eternity has begun. The more to come are those who are yet to know Him. Because eternity has no beginning but is here, from your perspective, it has begun. Because He is, We are eternal, and there is no time limit on the more to come.

"When the fullness of those who are to come is complete, the eternal Father will give the signal to raise the flag. For now, you and the others are buckled into eternity, awaiting eternity's signal. Because you are in eternity in Us, you can rest in knowing eternity has begun.

Peace, eternal peace like a river, floods my being. I feel the seat of the chair under me on the lanai and am moved back into the natural. Wow! What an amazing start to a new day.

"Thank You, Papa. Help me to live in the perspective of eternity today. Amen."

WEATHERED CARRIER

Today is Good Friday.

Last night, I asked Papa to get me up by 4:30 this morning.

At 4:20 my eyes pop open. "Time to get up," I say to myself.

I remain in bed for a few minutes, praising and thanking Him for the new day. "I bless You, Papa, for the day You have given me. Help me to use this day for Your glory."

Out on the lanai in my chair, I continue to give Him praise and honor. As I turn to partake of the communion elements, the words from a worship song start rolling through my mind.

"All hail, King Jesus! All hail the Lord of heaven and earth." The two lines repeat over and over in my mind. I'm focusing on Him and all He has made possible for me through His death, His shed blood, His mighty resurrection, and His gift of eternal life. As I do, the two lines in the song become reality.

"Jesus, You are the King. You are the Lord over heaven and earth. I bless You today. I thank You today for this reality. I thank You for conquering death and hell and coming back with the keys. I thank You for the new covenant in and through Your shed blood."

As I give thanks to Him, the spirit realm opens in front of me. Coming towards me on an angle from my left front is a person wearing the clothing of a person from the Middle East. The terrain looks barren and rugged. The person's head is shrouded. A long, flowing tan-colored garment wraps the person from head to just above the sandal-shod feet.

I see the face of a woman. A walking stick is in her right hand. It's long, and as she walks, the top of the stick or staff reaches just above her head. The staff looks big, and I sense it's not hers, but she is taking it to or carrying it for someone. In her left arm she is carrying a bundle close to her, like a small baby would be carried, tightly, next to her body. Her expression is very focused and determined.

As she gets closer to me, there is no eye contact. Her face looks young but also weathered. She is focused and continues at a steady pace past me. Then she disappears to my right, behind me. I feel a warm breeze blow past me as she as she passes on. It feels like the breeze is caused by her steady pace walking past me. I wonder.

Then I notice to my front left that she is coming again. Nothing is different. She passes and disappears. The same warm breeze blows over me. Again, I wonder. Then she comes towards me again, the same way for the third time.

As she walks towards me, I ask in my spirit, "Papa, what are You showing me? Can You please send Holy Spirit to explain?" I feel a whoosh of a cool breeze around me, and my body shakes. I feel as though I'm surrounded by His presence.

Through His presence, I see the woman has a different appearance. The determination is replaced with a smile. She pauses and looks at the presence surrounding me. This time she doesn't walk past me. She walks into His presence. She speaks a phrase in an unknown tongue. Understanding comes to me, and I know what she is speaking. Her words are, "I have been traveling the desert places of the earth looking for this presence." She lifts up the staff, and it is taken by Holy Spirit. Then she reaches to the bundle on her left, unrolling the garment to reveal a small, sleeping baby.

In the presence of Holy Spirit, the baby opens its eyes. The baby's eyes are a striking bluish green, almost aqua, color. The baby's dark, deep brown skin matches the woman's.

The staff she handed to Holy Spirit is glowing. He touches the baby's head with the staff and leaves it there. The staff leaning on the baby's head transfers the glow to the baby. The staff is removed, and the baby continues to glow. This glow causes the eyes to be transformed to a brilliant color in the midst of the white around the blueish aqua irises. The baby's eyes connect with Holy Spirit's eyes. I see a transfer Spirit to spirit as they connect, like light beams between the eyes.

Then, like a switch turning off, the light beams stop. The baby's eyes glance at me, and I feel an impartation of something with just a glance. Then the eyes close, and the glow of the baby's skin diminishes. The woman again says something in an unknown tongue and wraps the baby up again. She receives the staff back from Holy Spirit and lifts it in the air as a sign of thanks. Holy Spirit nods, and she walks out of His presence. Continuing her walk, she disappears behind me to my right. Again, I wonder and wait.

Understanding again comes to the words she spoke in an unknown tongue. The words are, "The impartation is good. The staff is purified. The baby will now live and will walk in true authority in the earth."

While still in His presence I ask, "Who is the woman? Who is the baby? Is she coming from somewhere specific and going to somewhere specific?"

I hear the voice of the Spirit of Knowledge speak. Whoa! I realize they are all here.

"Yes, We are," He says. "The woman though weathered and tired, is not weary. She has been carrying this baby for a long time. She has also been using His authority, the staff, to stay on her path. She has been looking for the presence of the Holy One. The father of the child wandered into exposure. In the exposure, she protected and carried the baby and the staff in hopes she would find His holy presence.

"Today she has wandered into His presence, and the baby will live and walk in its rightful authority. The woman is the Church. The baby is the true movement birthed in the wilderness of a castaway from an exposed movement. The authority given was misused, but the woman did not discard the staff of the authority. Holy Spirit has purified the staff of authority and touched it to the baby that it may live. The woman wrapped the baby to carry and protect it until maturity and time of revealing come. It will not die from exposure."

All is quiet around me. I wait and I wonder.

I hear, "You will be learning more about the warfare realm to protect the baby. Things will be heating up in the exposure to come."

This morning brings me to a state of intercession for the protection of the mother, the child, the Church, and for what has been birthed to come into maturity.

The Spirit of Knowledge nods towards the Spirit of Understanding and says, "Understanding will continue from here."

Understanding speaks in a calm voice, "There are times in history when what has been conceived has died. This is not the case with this child. Because the mother didn't abandon or abort the child, it will live. The life it has is not its own. This life has been protected by a caring mother. Now it has been infused with the life of the Spirit, and it will grow in the true identity of the Spirit. Actually, the wilderness of exposure will now be a wilderness of protection unto maturity. The Church is now carrying and protecting what has been birthed and the authority that has been birthed with it. The growth will happen quickly, and the authority will be undeniable.

"To answer the question in your mind, what has been birthed now exists but has not been seen in the earth before, either in manifestation or authority. You are to pray into this as you're prompted by Holy Spirit. Pray for true, pure maturity and that the authority will not be questioned. This authority will be challenged, and when it is challenged, the fullness of the authority will be revealed. The authority revealed will silence all the challenging. Truth is rising up like never before, and truth will have its way.

All is quiet again. I wonder and ponder. In this quiet, pondering wonder, I feel His presence dissipate, and I'm brought back into the natural realm.

"Papa, I know this wonder will stay with me. Please quicken my spirit, the ears and eyes of my spirit, to pray when You would have me pray. Amen."

SYIYA AND METAK

Today is the day in between the crucifixion and resurrection. As I pray into what I saw yesterday, I see a vivid picture of the mother holding the baby. She looks peaceful. Even the weathered look is faded, and her face appears youthful. She is receiving an overflow of the life in the baby.

For several minutes I pray for protection of the life in this child. Then I pray over and into the authority. "Papa," I pray, "let this authority, Your authority, not be questioned. I pray Your authority, Papa, grows in and through the child, the mother, Your Church and what You're doing in Your Church. Amen."

The scene in front of me expands, and I see the mother sitting in a chair next to a wall. The back of the chair is against the wall, and there are empty chairs to her right and to her left. She appears to be in a safe place, not an alone place. This place looks familiar to me. I hear a sound of footsteps and feel a presence behind me. The mother smiles and nods. I turn to see Sir standing behind me.

"Good morning, Colonel. Great to see you," he says.

He greets me with open arms, and we share a big hug. As we embrace, I see the others over his shoulder and realize I'm in the classroom. I think, "Wow, what a change in this man. The growth from bondage to freedom and maturity has been quick."

This thought triggers another thought. I was told the baby would grow quickly. In the spirit I pray, "Thank you, Papa, for this living example right in front of me of Your Spirit growing in a person submitted to You."

Sir points to the mother and child with an open hand and says, "I see you have met Syiya and her little boy Metak."

Turning, I respond while looking at her, "Yes, I have. We met yesterday. Although we were not formally introduced, we did meet. I see she is a very caring mother and has an amazing young man in her arms." I nod to her, and she nods back.

Sir says, "Yes, she seems like a good mother, very protective of the child though."

"Yes, some mothers are like that," I respond. I move towards Syiya to introduce myself, and she quickly rises from her seat. I say, "Hi, I'm Colonel, Syiya. Nice to meet you and Metak."

She responds by nodding her head and hands me the baby.

Sir says to me as I'm receiving the baby, "Wow, Colonel! She hasn't let anyone touch him. You must've made a very good impression on her when you met."

I respond to Sir, "We have a mutual friend who was with me when we met. I think because of that, she feels safe. When she realizes you all are friends of Holy Spirit, things will lighten up."

Sir responds, "Yes, He has a way with people."

I hold Metak cuddled into my left arm so that I can look at his face and into his eyes. I speak to him and say, "Yes, you are a handsome little guy. One selected and anointed of the Lord to initiate great things for Him in His kingdom. I bless you to be all that He has created you to be. I bless your mother to bring you to maturity."

Out of the corner of my eye I see Syiya smiling. I know she understands what I'm saying to Metak, even though English is not her first language. Metak's eyes open, and he looks directly into mine. I feel a deeper impartation of what I felt yesterday when he glanced at me. It feels amazing and wonderful.

Looking to Syiya, I say, "He is an incredible boy. I can see it in his eyes."

She quickly nods at my words. I feel the baby squirm a bit in my arms and know it's time to hand him back to her. She receives him back, nods, and sits back down. The staff is under her chair laying sideways.

I feel a presence and something heavy leaning on my left shoulder. I glance to see Holy Spirit standing there. The weight of His hand on my shoulder is so heavy I can hardly move.

He whispers into my spirit, "I just popped in to check on them," as He nods towards Syiya, who is totally attentive to the baby. She doesn't notice Holy Spirit.

He says to me, "No one in the room except you and the seven Spirits know I'm here. I wanted to tell you she has never given him to anyone before. You are the first, and it was not easy for her to do that. She saw you with Me in My presence yesterday and knows you're safe. She will see me here in the classroom and will realize We guided her here with Metak. Once she realizes this is a training place for him, she will release him into the fullness We have for what he will carry. Right now, she still needs to carry him. All in due time the release will happen. All in due time. He is a beautiful baby, isn't he?"

I feel the weight of Holy Spirit subside and then leave, as I respond to His question, "Yes, he is." I hear myself muttering, "All in due time. All in due time."

Sir says to me, "You talking to yourself, Colonel?"

I smile and nod towards Syiya and Metak and say, "No, I just felt led by the Spirit to pray for them."

Sir says, "Good. For a second there, I thought you might be listening to spirit voices like I used too."

I think, "He doesn't know how right-on his comment is. Not the voices he was listening to, but Holy Spirit."

Then Sir says, "I like how you are just led by Holy Spirit to pray in your spirit for someone. I'll need some training in that."

I respond with, "Yes, Sir, I believe that training is coming. All in due time. All in due time."

I feel a little awkward talking to Sir next to the mother and baby. I say to him, "Let's move over there." I motion with my hand to a place near the side, so Syiya can be alone with Metak. Sir complies, and we move to the side.

As we do, Sir says to me, "That was quite a connection you had with Metak. What's up with that?"

I hesitate and say back to him, "I believe Holy Spirit has a great plan for his life, just like He does for all of us." I nod back at Metak. "I'm glad to see them here, and I'm glad Holy Spirit brought them to the class like He brought you."

Sir says, "I thought you brought me into the class?"

I respond with, "Well I did, at Holy Spirit's direction. He brought me to you. Then you and I came here on the transport He provided." I can almost see the wheels spinning in Sir's mind for him to remember. There must still be some confusion to be washed out by the Word and the renewing of his mind. But I see he is definitely getting cleaned out by what's being taught in the class. While he's thinking, I pray in my spirit as I'm looking at him, "Papa, continue to clean out that confusion. Restore his mind and make it whole. I call on the finished work of Jesus over his mind. Amen."

Sir says, "Yes that's right. I remember now. He pulled me out of a bad place and invited me here. We met on the ride over."

"Yes, that's it," I respond. "By the way, how are things going for you here?"

"Delightful," Sir responds. "Everyone here is helpful and makes me feel special. Shama has been real good at answering questions and helping me along. I see there is still a lot to learn."

Then he says something I've heard my wife say as we've been in conversations with people.

He says, "It's like I heard Wisdom say in one class, 'There are things you have learned that you must unlearn so you can relearn.'"

His comment brings a smile to my face as I think of the blessed life I live with a wife who listens to Wisdom. I also look over his shoulder to see Wisdom looking at us as we speak. She nods and smiles back at me. I take this as a confirmation of my thought about my wife listening to Her.

Sir says, "I need to get back to class. We are finishing up this phase and moving into the next, which will be leadership training for the mission ahead." He gives me a hug, turns, and walks back to his class.

I pray in my spirit, "Bless him, Papa. Continue to bring him to the place you have for him and this team. Impart all they need for their trek across the bridge into the warfare realm. I know you will connect them with the right people there. Amen."

I feel the eyes of Syiya looking at me. I turn in her direction to see her sitting on a chair with Metak snuggled in. I nod to her and notice the staff under the chairs is glowing. Our eyes connect. She nods, and I drift out of the spirit and back to my chair on the lanai.

Pondering these last few days in and out of the spirit realm, I realize we are all on a great adventure with Him. It depends on us and how far we want to venture into His presence.

"I bless you, Papa. Thank You for taking me into the realms beyond the natural to be where You are. Amen."

TRAINING GROUND

I sit in my library chair while I'm standing in my spirit in the midst of a thick fog. I hear footsteps cautiously approaching behind me. My heart rate picks up. I don't speak aloud, but inwardly I begin to praise and thank Him for this day and where I am.

I reach up to put my hand on my chest to speak peace and to quiet my heart and spirit. My hand touches a pouch on my chest. I feel it and realize it's a quiver strapped to me. It occurs to me that this is for my weapons in the warfare realm. This is where I am. The steps I hear must be friendly. I speak in the spirit, "Knowledge, is that You approaching?"

I hear back in my spirit, "Colonel, you have learned well."

He appears through the fog, and I am so relieved. He salutes me by placing His hand on His chest, and I return the salute.

He continues Spirit to spirit, "You have learned that speaking and communicating in the spirit is also a weapon, not just in this realm, but in all realms."

I respond, "Thanks for that insight. I didn't realize this was a weapon."

"Yes, anything used as an advantage to overcome the enemies of our Lord and His body is a weapon against them. You have seen this first-hand many times. It now is a spiritual part of you, and you move in it naturally."

I think, "Wow, it is!" Then, the thought continues, "I just knew in my spirit not to speak aloud, and I didn't. I directed my spirit thoughts towards Knowledge, and He heard me in the Spirit."

"Yes," He responds, "and you did it naturally. You will keep hearing Me and the others saying this until it's confirmed deep in your spirit. So, your thoughts will naturally flow from your spirit, just as your heart beats and your lungs breathe."

When He says "heartbeats," I feel peace in my heart and realize the beating has slowed to a peaceful rate, with my breathing normal. This peace brings up a question in my spirit. I ask, "May I?"

He says, "Yes, by all means."

I say, "I directed my spirit words towards You when I asked, 'Knowledge, is that You?' Is this another weapon?"

With glee, He responds, "Yes, it is. If you think about it, communication in the spirit is powerful. General speech and blessing in the spirit are good, but when it's directed, it's more powerful. Just like in the natural, it's heard by the one it's directed towards. There is no echo, reverberation, or question as to who it's spoken to. Your speech, especially spirit-directed speech, is a weapon in this place and other realms."

"Communication spirit to Spirit does a few other things you have experienced. It keeps you hidden in Us or in Holy Spirit as you communicate. Also, it gives you the ability to move throughout the realms directed by the Spirit of the Lord, unnoticed while you move. Unnoticed and hidden are two different things. Hidden is a covering in a specific place. Unnoticed is being covered while you move from place to place. There may be movement in the spiritual realm, which can be felt by those sensitive in the spirit. But movement directed by the Father is unnoticed movement, even though it is felt in the spirit. It's felt but not seen. This does happen both ways. Sometimes you might feel an uneasy or uncomfortable feeling. This is the time to ask for discernment, and the Father will send Holy Spirit or one of Us to bring what's needed.

"You heard My footsteps in the spirit and knew in your spirit it was Me. This comes from spending time in His presence. He reveals Us in a way that makes it clear you are discerning Us."

He stops His teaching and says, "I see you felt that."

"Yes," I respond, "while you were talking, I felt a shift but thought it was You."

"Good observation," He says, "but if we are communicating face to face in the spirit, unnoticed and hidden, why would you think it's Me?"

I know He didn't ask me that question for an answer but as a teaching point for me to ponder. He continues, "I want you to focus on what you're feeling and ask for discernment."

I close my eyes to focus in this place; the fog dissipates. While in the spirit, I see a person being brought into the warfare realm. This person is connecting with another person who is already in this realm.

Knowledge breaks into my focus, "Good, good. Keep focusing. Zero in. Who do you see? Do you recognize the two people?"

I think, "This is good. His encouragement is helping me along."

I hear, "Don't think. Focus."

Man! Have I heard this statement before!

"Yes, you have," He says, "Focus. Don't wander in your thinking."

"Okay," I say. "A small person came in, and another slightly larger person who met them."

I hear again, "Yes, good. Can you see who they are?"

"Yes, it's Shama. Holy Spirit brought her in."

He says, "Yes, it is. Who is she with? Who met her?"

Continuing to focus on the two of them, I ask, "Father, please give me discernment and understanding." Immediately another presence enters the hidden place we are in. It's Understanding standing with us.

Understanding says, "Continue to focus. You know who the other person is. She has been with you before."

While continuing to focus, spiritual deduction takes place in the mind of my spirit, "This would not be Wisdom, although it could be? But I know it's not."

I hear both of them say, "Good. Good."

Then Understanding says, "Focus. What do you see? You know it's a female."

A flash of a sword catches my eye. "That's Carmon," I exclaim with a smile in my spirit.

"Yes, it is," They respond simultaneously.

Knowledge continues, "Shama is on a field trip, and Carmon is her mentor on the trip."

"Wow!" I think. "Couldn't have been a better pick for Shama." Outside our hidden place, I sense some movement and hear footsteps.

Knowledge says, "Welcome into Our hidden place."

Next, I hear a sound like a bubble stretching with a boing and a snap. Then the two of them appear with us. "This is so awesome," I say as I give Carmon a big hug, "My, how you have grown."

"Yessir, Colonel," she responds, "and you have also. I can see it in your spirit."

Pointing to them with both hands open, I say, "I'm overjoyed to see you, Carmon. It's wonderful that you have met Shama."

Shama chimes in, "It's great for me, Colonel, that I've met Carmon. She will be mentoring me for a short time here in this realm."

I look at her and say, like a proud daddy, "Yes, it is. She is a mighty warrior and a great mentor. She has a lot to impart to you in this realm.

Will you be here long?"

"I've been told as long as it takes, Colonel," Shama replies.

Carmon says, "I've been given intel from these Guys, pointing over her shoulder with her right thumb. Their intel is always right on. Wisdom also told me Shama is ready for field training, so here she is. This is a great place for one-on-one field training."

I'm a little concerned for these two young girls out here in the warfare realm.

"Don't worry, Colonel," Carmon says, "These Guys will be close by, and Wisdom is always above," as she glances up, "and, if need be, Might has our rear guard. Like I said, this place is a great training ground. Besides, Sir needs a good wing man, in this case, a girl, nodding at Shama. She has great skills. I've also been auditing their class, sharpening my skills, and observing who will be coming in.

"You three did awesome with Sir," looking first at me, "you, Colonel and Shama," as she nods her head towards her, "and Ollie. I like that kid. He's going to do great here as well."

I'm thinking, "Who is this girl, and what happened to the little Carmon I used to know?

She looks at me with those deep sky-blue eyes and says, "Now, now, Colonel, you said it yourself. I've grown. Some of that growth has come from observing you. Holy Spirit has had you in some pretty awesome training grounds yourself. The way you identified and revealed that bridge! Eyes of faith, Colonel, eyes of faith. You revealed the bridge and another weapon here in this realm for all of us. Eyes of faith, seeing what's there even if ya don't see it. Those eyes gained access for all of us."

I'm pretty overwhelmed at her observation. I'm at a loss for words. All I know is I'm glad I'm on her side.

Knowledge and Understanding say in unison, "Amen."

We all chuckle in the spirit. But Knowledge brings it home by saying, "There's more out there like her. More than you know. More than you know."

I say, "Wow, that sure builds hope."

Knowledge nods and says, "Yes, it does."

Nodding, I respond, "I know one thing for sure. Because of You guys, pointing to Knowledge, Understanding, and the Others, my prayer life has gone up another level or so."

They nod Their heads in gratitude, and Carmon says, "Yes, because of Them, all of us have grown in our reverent fear of the Lord." Without a pause she says, "Colonel, we have an assignment to get to. We will see you again soon."

Saluting from their hearts, they are on their way. Just like that, they are out of our hidden place and going unnoticed in the covering of the Lord.

I realize I've been using three more weapons: speaking spirit to Spirit, directed spirit speech, and eyes of faith.

And there's also being hidden versus being unnoticed. They are powerful in different ways in this and other realms.

There is a lot more to learn, and the training seems to have ramped up. "Must be You are up to something, Papa!"

I hear, "All in due time. All in due time."

The presence of Knowledge and Understanding fades, and I'm brought back into my chair in the natural. The smile in my spirit finds expression on my face as I think of what just transpired in the spirit realm.

"Wow, Papa! You are amazing. Thanks for connecting Shama with Carmon. It was good to see her again. Once more, I see Your plans are not our plans."

"I'm so thankful to You for this, Papa. Amen"

TWO GRAVES

For the last few days the chorus from a worship song has been rolling through my spirit. This morning it continues:

Lord, You are good and Your mercy endureth forever;
We worship You. We worship You, for You are good;
From generation to generation, we worship You;
Hallelujah, hallelujah,
You are good all the time. All the time You are good.

The other day, as I drove down the road with this chorus in my spirit, the spirit realm opened. I'm standing in a graveyard in front of two graves. The one on the left is mounded up, and the one on the right is freshly dug, open, and empty.

I say, "Lord, this looks like something You will explain to me while I sit and wait on You. Can You bring this back to me in the library?"

Then today, as I'm waiting on the Lord, the chorus still rolling through my spirit, I'm standing in front of the graves again. Just like when I was driving. The open one on the right and the mounded one on the left. Walking up closer to them, I notice the open grave is very deep. It's not bottomless, just very deep.

"Thank You, Papa, for bringing me back here today. Why are You showing me these two graves?"

In answer to my question, I'm brought back to a previous visitation with Him that I recorded in my book *Realm Walkers*, "Circle of Graves."

In that visitation, I was in a cemetery in the middle of a circle of graves. He is reminding me about that visitation. There He said, "The seven Spirits mentioned in Isaiah 11:2 assisted as I led you to one grave. Speak to that grave. They will guide you concerning what's in the grave that needs to be resurrected."

Getting back to the present, I pause and think of that statement, realizing it's all present with Him. I pray, "Father, I come before You in the Spirit of the Lord, as spoken of in Your word. May Your Spirit rest upon Your Son Jesus Who lives in me. I call my spirit forward to be out front to commune with You. I speak to my natural mind, will, and emotions to come into order behind my spirit. Please send Your Holy Spirit manifesting in the spirits of Wisdom and Understanding, Counsel and Might, and Knowledge through the Holy Fear of Your Spirit, the Spirit of the Lord. Amen."

The room fills with a thick, holy, reverent presence. With this presence in the room, the natural me feels very small. The chorus is still rolling through my spirit. I take this as a sign to worship, and I do. For several minutes I sit quietly, worshiping from my spirit to His, spirit to Spirit.

Through my worship to Him, I feel my spirit rise and become one with Him in this Holy presence.

The spirit of Wisdom speaks first, "We have been preparing your spirit by letting this worship chorus roll through your natural mind and your spiritual being. The saturation of this worship is creating this holy moment. In the span of eternity, this is only one holy moment, but moments in His and Our presence affect eternity. For decades the Church has been treating worship and praise as one, and that is not the case.

"When you worship a holy, omnipotent Creator, that truly is worship. Worship is directed to who He is, spirit to Spirit, not what He has done. Everything He does and has done flows out of who He is. Many people confuse the two and worship Him for His works and, therefore, praise Him amiss. Yes, praise can be given for who He is, but who He is deserves ultimate worship. So, you worship Him for who He is and praise Him for His goodness. Holy praise will flow from pure worship of who He is."

Wisdom defers to Understanding who says, "To answer the question you have about the graves. No, We are not here to resurrect anything about worship or praise. Sometimes Wisdom speaks relevant sayings and enigmas intended for a different time. We will leave that in your spirit for a later time.

"The two graves you are standing in front of are for you to speak to today."

I say, "May I ask a question?" Understanding agrees with a nod.

I continue, "There is a mounded grave and an open grave. Papa said I would speak to the graves to resurrect. How can something be resurrected from an open grave?"

"Great question. You will speak to a grave through the Spirit of Might." Understanding motions towards Might. He is in His typical position of arms crossed, leaning against an invisible wall. Might nods with a smile.

Understanding continues, "When you speak to the mounded grave through the resurrected power of Jesus in the Spirit of Might, the counterfeit or the false assumed doctrine will be buried in the open grave next to it and covered over. The graves that are opened from what will be resurrected do not get filled in. They are like the empty tomb Jesus laid in. They remain open as an eternal memorial to what has been resurrected. Understand that you in and of yourself are not resurrecting anything. This is the Spirit of the Lord working through a submitted vessel by means of the Fear of the Lord. Even Jesus did not resurrect Himself. It was the Father's doing."

I respond to Understanding with, "I understand."

Understanding nods to Knowledge, who says, "Now that We have proper order established, We will proceed. Over the years, the grave to the left has been gradually filled, and its contents have been covered over.

Things put there by false teaching and doctrines of men, justified by beliefs established by the false teachings.

"The resurrection is a combination of two things working hand in hand with the Lord. Like Understanding said," as He nods towards Her, "the open grave on the right will be for the counterfeit, the false teaching. The counterfeit will not be seen for what it is until the real is resurrected and restored. So, the open grave on the right may stay open for a while until the covering is complete. Holy Spirit will work with Might to cast the other false doctrine into the grave, but the Church will need to fill it in and cover it up. As the true doctrine replaces the belief system of the counterfeit in the Church, the covering will happen. Once the true doctrine becomes established, the false will be truly seen for what it was and the damage it did. This will keep it in the grave.

"Through the training you have received about the weapons used in the warfare realm, you can speak to the grave through Us. The process of listening and being led by Us is critical, as you have learned.

"Since mankind has put this doctrine from the Lord in the grave assisted by the spirit or spirits of the evil one, it must be raised through a man being assisted by the Spirits of the Lord through the Fear of the Lord. Are you getting this?" Knowledge asks.

I nod my head and realize my natural mind agrees with my spirit in this process. I feel anticipation growing in my being and spirit.

Knowledge continues, "Yes this is a spiritually natural thing we are about to engage in."

Next, I feel a cold wind on my back. Knowledge calls, "Might, step in."

He does, and I feel the wind subside. Knowledge says, "The wind is the spirit of doubt trying to blow confusion over you and your natural mind. Don't let this happen."

I take this as a cue to empower my spirit by praying in tongues. I've learned in class I'm to pray, guided and led by the Spirit. I feel the protection of Might in this process. With His protection from the wind, I hear a howling in the spirit.

Knowledge speaks to this as well, "Command your ears to be tuned to hear the chorus in your spirit. Worship Him! Worship Him!"

When I do that, one part of the chorus, "from generation to generation," becomes louder in my spirit than the howling in my ears.

"Good. Good. You're following Our leading and guidance," I hear from Knowledge.

I feel a tremble in my body, like I'm being shaken and hit from the outside. I hear Knowledge call out, "Rise up, Spirit! Rise up, Spirit of the Lord, over this process." I feel a covering like a blanket rest over me. I can still feel slight bumps and bangs, but know I'm covered from the attack.

"Okay," Knowledge says, "Now they will attempt to attack your mind. Stand up in the knowledge of who you are in Christ. Call on your identity of who you are in Him and who He is in you. They are trying to attack your authority as a believer in the most high God and what He has done for you through the shed blood of His Son. Step into who you are and let Might speak through you to open and raise what's in this grave."

I feel a swelling in my spirit and a clarity in my mind as I'm being led and following Knowledge's instructions. Words form deep within my being and start to come from the depths of my spirit. A roar comes out of my mouth like I've never heard before. The words are unintelligible to my natural mind, but my spirit approves. Then I see a crack in the earth covering the grave, and a bright light begins to shine through the crack. More cracks appear.

Understanding comes to bring understanding, "Through the Spirit of Might, you are calling forth what's been buried. You are calling forth a resurrection of holy boldness back into the Church. Continue to speak. Call it forth. Use the authority you have through Jesus and His name. Step into and step out in the holy boldness you are calling forth."

I continue to do as They say. Speaking boldly through the spirit, I see a shining light appearing over the grave that was covered but is now opened. I'm almost blinded, and I know I need to look through spiritual, not natural, eyes. The light of His holiness causes me to bend at my waist and then hit the ground in His presence. I hear thunder roll through the space I'm in.

Understanding says, "The forces that were trying to hinder you have been pushed back by the holy boldness released."

Knowledge comes back into the lead, picks me up, and says, "Now it's time to call out the counterfeit and cast it into the pit of the open grave on the right."

I feel a slap on my back, and again words start to form deep in my spirit. He says, "That's Might, giving your spirit a boost." Once more, the words roll out of me in mighty tongues like the thunder I just heard. A gray, fierce-looking storm cloud moves over me.

"Speak to the storm," I hear in my spirit.

I raise my head, and tongues of thunder come up from my spirit again, directed to the cloud. Liquid like rain begins falling on my face.

I hear in my spirit, "Distractions from the cloud. Pay it no attention."

I continue to speak out in tongues. I see and feel a clear shield cover my face and body. My words go through, and the raining distractions from the cloud are repelled. My right arm rises, and I look at it as it rises. It's pointing to the open grave. The cloud starts to break apart. Pieces of it fall off and into the grave.

Understanding comes again and says, "The cloud of arrogant pride can't cover or replace the rightfully released holy boldness. It was formed bit by bit by false teaching, and, bit by bit, it is falling into the grave."

The last bits of the cloud drop out of the sky and into the grave. The sky seems to clear.

Understanding says, "Call out truth through holy boldness to rise up in the land. As you call out truth, the Church will begin to fill the grave in to cover the fallen false doctrine."

I hear my voice ring out into the atmosphere, "Truth, I call you forth to speak through holy boldness. Come forth and take your rightful place to cover this false doctrine." Dirt is shoveled into the grave, covering the false doctrine.

Knowledge comes back and says, "We led you as We were led by Holy Spirit. You are a willing vessel, and all this brings glory to the Father. A resurrection has taken place, and a burial is in process. It will continue as truth grows throughout the land. Keep on praying in the fear of the Lord for the full manifestation of this. Well done with the first grave."

I'm undone at His comment to me.

Wisdom comes with a soothing voice to wrap things up, "I will be here as a covering sent by the Father. Knowledge and Understanding are to your right and left, with Might as your rear guard. Keep your eyes on the Lord and rest in the truth that this moment in eternity has been recorded."

All is quiet and still. An overwhelming peace fills the room and covers me. The chorus is still rolling through my being with worship on my lips and in my spirit to Him Who Is.

Wow, what a day! Selah.

Pondering all this today, I realize Papa used me in a significant way for His glory.

"Help me to remain a submitted vessel to be used by You, Papa. Amen."

SING A LITTLE LOUDER

A different chorus is going through my spirit this morning:

I sing a little louder,
In the presence of my enemies.
I sing a little louder.
Hell has lost its hold on me.

A blessing comes up in my spirit to bless the United States. First, I repent for national pride being more valued than Christian liberty. I realize we have this nation because of Christian liberty. It's not the other way around.

While I pray, one part of the chorus repeats over and over in my spirit:

Sing a little louder.

This is the focus for several minutes of prayer.

Shifting into the spirit, I'm back in the cemetery. This place feels like death, not life, but I don't see graves. Instead of graves, a row of thrones is situated in front of me. The thrones are empty. I feel they represent a combined authority. There are six thrones.

Then a large right foot comes down and crushes them, all at the same time. The crushed thrones are then kicked aside and disappear. In their places, six more thrones rise out of the earth. These six have people sitting on them. I feel arrogance and pride coming from them. This is the same thing I called out and cast into the grave previously.

As I focus on them, "sing a little louder" keeps rolling through my spirit. As I sing in my spirit, wings from heaven attached to invisible bodies swoop down and remove the people from the thrones. I think these are heavenly beings sent from the Father to remove them, but maybe more clarity will come later.

All six are removed at the same time by these invisible bodies, one for each person. I see two of the people struggle. One person doesn't struggle, but a stream of foul, rotten profanity flows from his mouth. The other three remain arrogant, even as they are being lifted off their thrones and carried away. Six empty thrones remain.

As I focus on the thrones, I feel a presence approaching me. It's not a bad or evil feeling; it's like a disturbance in the atmosphere around me. In my spirit I ask, "Papa, what's going on here? Do You have something You want to reveal to me? What is the presence I feel?"

Turning towards the approaching presence, I see Sir walking up to me with a hand over his mouth. I see no arm attached to the hand; it's just a hand, but not his. I think back to the first time Holy Spirit guided me into and through the enemy's camp. Sir's eyes are really big and bulging because of where he is and what he's seeing. He sees me and stops.

I look at him and speak in the spirit to his spirit, "Sir, can you hear me?"

He looks at me in wonder. There's almost a blank stare on his face. I repeat in the spirit, "Sir, can you hear me?" His gaze has been fixed on the thrones.

He turns towards me, and I ask again, "Sir, can you hear me?" His head nods up and down.

"Good," I respond in a peaceful and calm tone with my words coming slowly. "I know you feel a hand over your mouth. I see it also. This is not because you are being punished or restricted like you have been in the past. This is for our protection." I see peace covering him, starting to change his countenance. His eyes are not bulging like they were.

I say, "Holy Spirit has brought you here. In this place we need to communicate spirit to spirit. Any words you speak out in the natural will cause a disturbance in the atmosphere of this place. Do you understand me?"

He nods and points to the thrones, as Holy Spirit's hand is removed from his mouth.

I respond, "Sir, I see them also."

I pray in my spirit, "Papa, I need a little help here; please guide me in this."

I feel another Presence next to us. Looking at Sir, I know he feels it, too. His eyes are telling me he is uncomfortable with everything going on. Interestingly, in my spirit I hear the sound of a dial adjusting, like on a car radio. Next, I hear, "Hey, can you hear me?"

"Yes," I respond to Understanding in the spirit.

"Good," I hear back, "I have changed the channel, so Sir doesn't hear our conversation. He knows I'm here but can't see me. The three of us will communicate together in a minute, but you need some instructions first."

"I'm all ears," I respond.

He says, "We knew you would be. Holy Spirit has instructed Us that Sir needed to get to this realm for training, and He wanted you to do this part. You have learned to speak, to move, and to go with Our Spirit, and you have what Sir needs. You will need to impart to him what We have imparted to you. We will be here to guide you through the process with him. Lean into Us as much as you need. Some things he won't tell you, mostly because of the pain of his past. Other things he just hasn't learned how to communicate yet. He is a little apprehensive because he is not in the classroom where he encountered so much liberty. Bringing him here has caused some memories to surface that need to be dealt with. This is where you come in. You will be able to relate to him just as he needs.

"When we took Shama out of the class for her field training, he felt like he lost a friend. We will arrange a connection here in this realm for him to see her also. Continue to speak to him calmly, but be direct. He can handle it.

"Colonel, you have the deer-in-the-headlights look. Are you with Me?"

"Yes, yes, I hear You. My natural mind is trying to interrupt me with a process on how to do this."

Understanding sternly says, "Colonel, get out of your mind and into the spirit. This is a spirit training lesson, not a natural one. You will be imparting what you have learned from Us, spirit to spirit. You can do this--your spirit to his. We've got you--Our Spirit to yours. Don't force the impartation. Lean into Us to impart what he needs through you. We have an open channel to him and you and another open channel to you and Us.

I hear a frequency change and realize I'm back on the same spirit frequency as Sir.

"Colonel, can you hear me?" Sir says to me in the spirit.

"Yes, I can," I reply.

He says, "For a minute there, you had the deer-in-the-headlights look."

"Yes, I was in deep thought about something. Please forgive me for the drift."

"No worries, Colonel. You were right by my side all the time. You didn't go anywhere."

I reply with, "Yeah, just on a different frequency for a minute there."

"So, Colonel," he says, "where are we? Holy Spirit told me we were going for a ride. He mentioned something about a road trip and said you would know. I've gotten to know Him better since I've been in the

SING A LITTLE LOUDER

classroom. He's pretty cool. I really like Him. Not as scary as when I first saw Him."

I respond with, "Well, He mentioned a road trip to you?"

"Yup, sure did."

I smile and say, "We'll get to that. First things first. We are in a place called the warfare realm."

"Warfare realm," Sir responds with heightened interest. I see a hand on his mouth. His eyes begin to focus on his mouth.

"Yes, warfare realm, and Holy Spirit slipped His hand over your mouth because you were going to speak out naturally."

He nods, and Holy Spirit removes His hand. Sir says, "I guess this will take some practice."

"Yes, it will," I reply. "I have gotten to the point where I'll even put my own hand on my mouth at times. There will come a time when we will be free to speak in the natural, but we have some work to do first. The work here will not be done through our natural efforts. It will be done by submitting to the leading of Holy Spirit Who is following the leading of the Father. Holy Spirit will guide and direct us Himself or through one or all of the seven Spirits of the Lord. I know you have experienced the Spirit of Wisdom teaching in the classroom."

Sir says, "Yes. At first, I wondered why she was so pretty, if not downright beautiful. But the more I listened to Her teach and explain things and then defer to Understanding or Knowledge, I saw how really beautiful they all are. Not like the spirits that taught me where I used to be. Kind of like this place," as he moves his arms around, "This place...you called it the warfare realm, right?"

"That's correct," I respond and nod my head.

He continues, "This place's like the place I was in. Feels the same. They both give me the creeps."

157

"Why's that?" I ask.

He says, "It's just so dark and foggy, and I don't feel life here."

"Those are all good answers," I say. "That's why we are here, to bring light, to help clear up the fog and bring life."

Sir says, "Yeah, but, Colonel, it's like the spirits here rule this place."

"That's another reason we are here," I say. "They have taken this place by false authority. We are here to redeem it back to its rightful owner, the Lord."

I see in his eyes he wants to believe. I know he has some trauma to overcome. "Please help me, Papa," I pray.

I hear the frequency change, and Understanding says, "Do a class review. Talk about Holy Spirit and the Father."

Looking into Sir's eyes, I say, "I believe I understand. But I know you can help me in the areas I don't have full understanding or knowledge."

Sir raises his eyebrows, and he says, "Me help you? How am I going to do that, Colonel?"

I say, "Let's do a little class review."

Sir nods his agreement.

"Good. Let me think. You have seen and felt the power of the Holy Spirit in a good way, right?"

He nods.

"You felt the peace and righteous instruction through the Spirits of the Lord, right? And you learned from Them about the goodness of the Father, true?"

He nods again and says, "Uh huh."

"Great, and you have also learned the only reason you felt scared of

Holy Spirit was because you felt His holiness when you were controlled by the evil spirits. Now that you know Him for who He is, you like Him. You said it yourself."

He nods.

I feel Understanding nudging me to take a deeper and more personal approach with Sir. I nod to Him in agreement.

I say to Sir, "Can we pray quietly in the spirit? Remember, we can't naturally speak our words here. I'm feeling now is a good time to pray and ask for the Spirit of Understanding to come and lead us to understand why you're feeling like this."

Sir nods in agreement to pray.

I pray, "Father, we boldly come to you through the shed blood of Jesus, Your Son. We thank You for what He did for us. We thank You, Jesus, for going to a place far worse than this for us to redeem us and set us free. Through this authority, we ask for the Spirit of Understanding and any of the Others to come and guide us in the freedom You, Father, have for us. Amen."

Sir also says, "Amen," in agreement. At his agreement Understanding and Knowledge manifest next to us. Sir seems startled, and I see Holy Spirit's hand on his mouth. He says in the spirit, "I wasn't expecting them to show up in this place."

Understanding says, "What better place is there for Us to show up?"

Knowledge says, "This is where We need to show up. In places like this We can truly manifest the Spirit of the Lord."

Wisdom says, "Let's keep it on a stealth mode while We are here. For now, We or they," as She points to us, "don't want to draw any undue attention."

She says to Sir, "Sir, how can We help you in this place?"

I begin to pray in the spirit. I see Them softly shining.

Sir hesitates but says, "I just want it all gone. All the bad memories, all the control and torture. I want it gone. I want to walk in freedom in this place, just like the freedom I felt in the class." He points to the ground, as if he's referencing where he is.

Knowledge says to me on a separate frequency, "There it is, Colonel. Pray into a release of these memories. Call for true freedom and peace to flood his being."

I pray these words in the spirit with my eyes open.

Sir's eyes get bigger, and we hear a muffled grunting in the fog not too far from us. "I speak peace into your spirit, Sir. Receive His peace. The sounds you hear are real, but they can't touch you. You have been bought by the blood of Jesus. They feel a disturbance, but that's all they feel. They don't know we are here. Receive His peace. Release your fear and the memories of torture and control. Release the bad memories and the shame associated with them. I accept you, Sir. Jesus accepts you. Holy Spirit accepts you. And the Father accepts you. Release those bad memories and accept Their love for you."

Sir slowly raises his hands in the air. Tears flow from his eyes, down his cheeks, and over the hand of Holy Spirit as they drip to the ground. Each tear drop shakes the ground as it hits. I hear shrieks in the fog. Sir is lost in Their presence and doesn't hear the shrinks. I'm seeing freedom coming to him.

Understanding says, "It's the power of redemption hitting the ground. They," as He points out into the fog, "feel the shaking, and that's causing the shrieks." Pointing back to Sir, "His tears are going to be a catalyst for redeeming this place."

Sir's countenance changes right in front of me. I thought he was free, but now I know he is.

"I praise You, Papa, for another soul truly set free."

Looking past Sir, I see the six empty thrones.

Understanding says on the private frequency, "We will get to them. We needed to take care of this first. Only free men can help men become free. We needed him free."

Basking in the joy of the moment, I'm brought back to my library chair. What started a few days ago has come to complete freedom for Sir. I know I'll be back here to talk about the thrones.

Holy Spirit whispers, "You can count on it. We need you and Sir back here. For now, sleep on it."

I'm excited about getting back to this place with Sir. I know we will get understanding and meet up with Carmon and Shama in the process.

I hear, "You can count on it. Each time you come, you can sing a little louder."

"Help me to sing in my sleep, Papa, and bring me back soon. Amen."

RIGHTFUL HEIR

It's still dark outside when I get to my library chair this morning. In the natural I hear a distant train horn. I'm brought into the spirit realm to the sound of a horn blowing. As I turn to where the sound comes from, I get a glimpse of the thrones. Seeing them, I feel as though I'm not alone.

I'm not. I hear a conversation in the spirit realm.

Understanding chimes in, "That's Sir talking with Shama."

I think, "If Shama is here, then Carmon must be here also."

"Yes, sir, Colonel, I'm here," a familiar voice says from beside me.

"Carmon!" I exclaim. "Holy Spirit said we would be seeing you here. I'm thankful for His faithfulness. How's it going?"

"Going real good, Colonel. Shama is amazing."

I see her look towards where Shama and Sir are talking. Holy Spirit has His hands on both of their mouths.

Carmon chuckles, "Yes, it really is a learned way of communicating, spirit to spirit."

"Yes, it sure is," I respond. "So what have you two been up to while here?"

"We've been doing some exploring," she says. "Lots of strongholds in this place, nothing too big for the Lord though."

I'm reminded of Caleb's statement about taking the mountain after they had crossed into the Promised Land and took the land. He had a daughter to whom he awarded the upper and lower springs after he got his promised territory.

"Yes, sir, Colonel," she says. "That's the lineage I come from. Mighty warriors in my lineage."

I'm amazed but not surprised at her comment.

Carmon then takes a slight step in front of me and points to my left. I look to where her right arm and open hand are pointing to see the thrones. She says, "Past those empty thrones is an area of deep darkness. It's like the darkness is behind the influence of the thrones. That's the place that needs to be taken in this realm. If we believe the Lord," she bends at the waist when she says 'the Lord,' "has established the authority in this place, then we know that evil has been drawn to His authority to try to take it. The thrones were put here by Him. He is the rightful owner. Anything or anyone occupying them that doesn't glorify Him must be dethroned."

Wow, the insight she has on the thrones is incredible.

Understanding speaks into our conversation. I see Carmon nod to Her as She speaks. She points to Carmon and says, "She has been in this and many other realms. She has good eyes to see through the fog of the evil one. She has seen how We have conquered in the past and knows We will conquer here. Once the teams are in place, the evil will be displaced."

This brings a question to my spirit. Understanding says, "What is it, Colonel?"

I say, "Thanks for allowing me to ask."

She nods.

I continue, "Holy Spirit said we were needed here, me and Sir," as I glance to where he is talking with Shama. "What's our mission here?"

She responds, "We will get to that when we have the four of you all together here." Pointing to Sir and Shama, Understanding continues, "Holy Spirit is causing the spirit connection to go deep between those two, like a true father, daughter connection should be. And, no, to the question in your mind. Sir is not her natural father. This is spirit to spirit. We need to keep the spiritual battles in the spirit. Remember, We bring the spirit into the natural, not the other way around."

While we are waiting, I ask for a pause to get on with my day.

She says, "When they are done," pointing to Holy Spirit, Sir, and Shama, "we will come back."

I didn't realize our pause would be a couple days.

This morning upon waking up, I'm drawn back into the warfare realm. Sitting in my library chair, I mentally wander into the cares of the day. I pray into those, one being my brother-in-law having bypass surgery this morning.

After prayer and communion, I feel a peaceful Presence fill the library and cover me in my chair. I know I'm back in the warfare realm, standing next to Carmon and looking towards the thrones. A young man wearing a small crown and a red robe walks up to one of the thrones. He stops and looks at them.

We hear his thoughts. He thinks pridefully, "Why are there six? I'm the rightful king. Who are these for?"

Carmon whispers into my spirit, "He won't last long. Too much pride."

I don't speak, just nod in agreement. The young man takes a throne near the center and sits down. He looks to his right and left and thinks, "They'll know I'm in charge. I got here first."

Then another young man walks up. He doesn't even pay attention to the man already sitting. He too seems to be filled with pride and takes a throne to the left of the first one, but leaves a seat open between them. His thoughts exhibit his pride also as he sits pompously, ignoring the man on the other throne.

I say to Carmon, "He won't last long either. Full of pride also."

She says, "Yes," as she looks into the dark fog. "I see another is coming," pointing off to her left.

I'm amazed at her vision. She saw this man coming long before I saw him. "Papa, please sharpen my vision in the spirit to see like that."

Carmon says, "He will, Colonel. Your spiritual sight has increased since our first meeting. It's like speaking spirit to spirit, a learned method of seeing. The more you practice, the more you see."

The third man walks up to the thrones. He stands several feet in front of them and the two men already seated. They both look at him with pride while we hear their thinking. "Well, are you going to sit, or are you here to bow before us?"

"Wow, what arrogance," I think.

Carmon nods at my thoughts.

The third man steps to the empty throne between the two men. They watch him as he kneels before the empty throne. He begins to pray. The other two quickly look away from him like they want nothing to do with him or his prayers. He doesn't pay any attention to them.

We hear his prayer, "Father, I'm thankful for this position. Help me to glorify You in it." A glowing bubble appears around him and surrounds him and the throne. Off past the thrones, I see eyes rising out of the darkness to see what's happening.

Carmon says, "His spoken prayers are causing a disturbance. We need to cover him in the spirit with prayer."

I hear her pray in the spirit and join in. Before long I hear prayers in tongues joining our prayers. I feel a person next to me and look to see Sir and Shama have joined us in prayer.

Sir leans over and says, "Holy Spirit said we needed to join you in prayer over this one. He is the one who will make way for Metak. This is Metak's grandfather. His son, Metak's father, was killed in battle against evil in another realm. Holy Spirit called it the realm of confusion."

I feel a wave of authority hit me when he tells me this. I increase my prayer in the spirit. While we are all praying with our eyes open, I see our prayers providing a spirit covering over this man. It's like clear waves leave us and cover him.

Then a dark gleam comes from eyes behind the thrones, looking our way. It's the darkness that rose up. It feels confused as to why its power is being challenged and pushed back. It feels it but doesn't see it.

Sir says, "Holy Spirit only said," as he points to the man on his knees, "he is the rightful heir to the throne. But he must fight for it, and we are here to help."

After the rightful heir prays, he glorifies the Father with raised hands and then stands.

He doesn't take the throne. He reaches into some type of pocket within his purple robe covering. His right hand comes out with a small flask. He removes the top. He begins to walk around the throne, pouring out a red liquid from the flask on the ground around the throne. The earth shakes under our feet. An evil shriek comes from the darkness. The flask doesn't run dry as he walks around the throne and pours out the continuous flow of red liquid. The rumbling continues.

The other two who are seated have their eyes closed and their hands over their ears.

Carmon is smiling. I hear her thoughts, "He did it; he actually poured out the wine as a sign of the blood around the throne. He dedicated it to the Father. This one is worthy of fighting for."

The rightful heir now stands in front of the throne with his back towards us. He reaches into the robe to return the flask, and his hand comes out with another smaller flask. With his right thumb, he pops open the top and lifts it to pour the liquid out. A clear liquid with a golden hue flows from this flask onto the left arm of the throne. He tips it up and does the same to the right arm of the throne. Then with his left hand open, he pours some of the liquid into the palm of his left hand. The liquid seems never-ending, just like the liquid in the first flask.

He closes the flask and places it back into his robe. Then he rubs the liquid from his left hand into his right. It drips through his fingers onto the seat. He reaches up to the top headrest of the throne and wipes the liquid over the head of the throne. Again, Carmon is smiling, and I hear her thoughts. "The pure anointing oil from the olive grove of the Lord. This throne is anointed for kingship."

The man steps back from the throne and bows his head towards the throne. He then turns towards us and bows his head, placing his right hand on his heart.

I'm thinking, "He can see us?"

I hear Understanding speak into my spirit, "He can see all of us. They can't," as She points to the other two who are still covering their ears with eyes closed. "But more importantly, they can't either," as She nods past the thrones.

I see confusion covering the evil behind the thrones. We return heart salutes. When the man drops his hand, I see a stained glowing imprint of the oil on his robe.

I hear Understanding in my spirit, "A heart anointed for eternity."

I think, "Wow," as I nod. The heads of those around me are nodding also.

The man doesn't sit; he walks away from the throne that's dedicated and anointed for the future king.

Sir says, "Yes, there is hope for this realm. It doesn't feel so yucky like it did at first."

I see a sheath attached to his chest with golden straps and his feet shod with golden soles. I realize he too has been gifted with the weapons needed to battle in this realm.

Carmon grabs my right hand and says, "Colonel, the battle is the Lord's. The gift is Him letting us be part of it with Them," her thumb goes over her shoulder, pointing to the seven Spirits around us.

"That," pointing to the confused evil, "has already lost."

Smiling at Carmon and Shama, Sir says to me, "I'm amazed at the wisdom of these two young warriors."

The four of us are engulfed by the seven Spirits, and I'm placed back in my library chair. The mist and the fog of the warfare realm are replaced by the sun shining through the window of a new day in the natural.

I ask, "Papa, please sharpen my spiritual sight to see what You have for me to see. Amen."

FREEDOM IN AND OUT OF DARKNESS

Before communion this morning, I'm moved back into the warfare realm. I'm still standing with the others in front of the thrones. Two are occupied; another is dedicated and anointed. The other three are unoccupied. A cart or wagon being pulled by two very ugly beasts comes out of the deep darkness behind the thrones.

The beasts look familiar. I have a flashback to what I saw in an encounter two years ago when a witch was riding a beast.

As the scene in front of me expands, I see a right hand holding reins like one would hold the reins of a horse. Looking down to the end of the reins, I see this is not a horse the witch is riding on. It's not a broom either. She is riding on some type of beast, the likes of which I have never seen before. It's very big and muscular. In comparison to its size, it has short, stocky legs and a flattened face on the head. Patches of shaggy, matted hair cover parts of this beast. On other parts, the hair is short and almost smooth. The witch and the beast are both ugly.

This beast moves with a slow, prideful cadence. The witch sits straight up in a prideful fashion. The beast's short, small ears are stuck close into the sides of its head. The big, pointed teeth protrude out of the sides and front of the mouth, with drool hanging from the bottom jaw. Every so often, as it continues to move forward, the head turns to the left and then back towards the right. When it looks in my direction, I see the eyes of this beast are totally black. I am careful not to connect with the beast's eyes.

This wagon or cart is moving slowly, and the driver is totally covered in black. I hear praying next to me. Carmon, Sir, and Shama are seeing and feeling all this and have taken it to the Lord in prayer. We, along with the Seven, are in a protective bubble provided by Holy Spirit. It feels like a secure bunker. We continue to observe and pray.

Carmon prays for continued covering. Sir and Shama have their hands over their mouths to keep their prayer in the spirit. Sir's eyes are wide open, like he recognizes some of the scene in front of us.

I ask, "Papa, can we get understanding of what's transpiring in front of us?"

Understand and Wisdom come to our aid.

Wisdom speaks first, "All of what is happening is for the ultimate demise of the darkness in this realm. Until the workers of darkness come out of their covering of darkness, they continue to move, covered by it. They are bringing their choices for the three remaining empty thrones."

Understanding speaks next. "If you focus on the cart the beasts are pulling, you will see a seat where the three demonic entities sit."

As I focus, the one dedicated throne disappears.

Sir says, "Where did the dedicated throne go?"

Carmon says, "Hey, guys, the throne is still there, but it's invisible to the demonic entities. They will not even attempt to sit in that throne, and they will not have that opportunity."

"That's right," Understanding says, "and the power emanating from it would cause them to turn around, run back into the darkness, and not come near it. We have covered it in the spirit so they can't see it."

As Understanding says this, my eyes are opened in the spirit, and I see the spiritual covering over this throne and the ground around it. The covering looks like a rolling waterfall of a transparent cloud. The waterfall seems to be going into the ground around it and replenishing itself through the throne. Understanding says, "You asked for clearer, sharper spiritual vision. The Father has answered your prayer."

Carmon smiles and says on a secure spirit frequency, "I heard that. It's almost like He said to you, 'Vision granted.' Keep leaning in, Colonel. There is more to see."

As I focus in on the cart and the entities on it, I see the cart resembles a bad counterfeit copy of something authentic royalty would ride in. There is nothing royal about this cart.

Understanding says, "They think they have the best. Because they are so blind, this cart appears royal to them."

At this point Knowledge takes over. He thanks Understanding and Wisdom for leading out in this. He looks at us as if we are in the classroom, and He is our teacher. "Good observation, Colonel. After all, this is field trading. And if We don't teach you what's here," pointing towards the cart coming in, "We can't train you on how to fight it."

The frequency changes so He can speak to Carmon and me. "Now We are going to open all your eyes to see what's riding in the cart. Colonel, get close to Sir so you can grab him. Opening his eyes to this may cause a flashback. Carmon, you got Shama. Strengthen her in the spirit."

Carmon moves so close to Shama they look like one in the spirit. Seeing this, I move in tight next to Sir and say, "This won't be pretty."

Wisdom also speaks so only Carmon and I can hear, "You two are seeing what's in front of you. Sir and Shama are feeling it but haven't seen it all yet. They have been praying against the feeling, while being encouraged by your prayer. Knowledge is about to open their eyes to see. They will first see the beasts, then the cart, then the driver, then the entities. Help them to be strong in the spirit. We are only showing them what they can handle as We expand the scene in front of them."

Carmon nods as I'm nodding. I hear the crack of a whip and feel Sir flinch next to me. His body starts to tremble and shake.

"I've got you. I'm right here," I say to him.

He responds, "Colonel, I'm not sure I can handle this."

I affirm him, "I'm right here. We are covered by Holy Spirit and the Seven."

I hear cart's wheels rolling over the rugged surface leading to the thrones, and the beasts come into view. It's like I see all this on a split screen. On one side, I see the whole scene, and, on the other, I see the expanding scene Sir is viewing.

"Yes," Knowledge says, "We have done this so you can track with Sir and what he sees.

Sir leans into me and says, "I've seen this before. The cloaked driver is not good. He only brings evil. Those beasts only do his bidding."

Looking at the beasts, I see them shake their heads, and drool flies left and right. This irritates them, and they seem to want to fight each other. The whip cracks again to bring them back in line. It seems to work.

Sir says anxiously, "They are approaching the dedicated throne. They will contaminate it."

I answer, "Let's pray into that."

"We are on it, Colonel," I hear Carmon say. Sir starts praying with an authority I haven't heard come from him before. Even Carmon looks up at him, smiling and nodding affirmation.

Sir says in the spirit, "Father, we invoke Your power and the Spirit of Might to pray through us. We proclaim You are the rightful authority in this place and that," as he points towards the cart, "cannot take any authority from that anointed throne."

I feel the power of his prayer and see it go out from him. The wave of his prayer joins with the covering of the anointed throne; the covering receives it and is strengthened by it.

Knowledge speaks into this like a teacher, "The Father is all powerful and all sufficient. He receives the prayers of His people and manifests through them. He is increasing the invisible power over that throne to keep it holy."

It also seems there is an increased power behind our prayers. Understanding directs our vision to the right of the thrones. The rightful heir is standing there with his arms raised, joining us in spirit-led prayer. I feel a presence behind us, too. The covering over us has somehow strengthened. Understanding says, "The combined prayer is doing this. If it wasn't for the Father concealing you in it, you all would be seen by the darkness."

Knowledge opens more of the scene in front of us. The beasts stop as they approach the thrones. The driver cracks the whip again, and Sir flinches. The sound of the whips cracking over and over causes Sir to put his hands over his ears. His body trembles.

I comfort him with a hug and tell him, "You are safe under the covering of the Father."

He mumbles to me in a shuddering, trembling voice, "I was in a cart like that. We were taken and forced to do the works of evil. The only way it got easier was to comply. We had to do some evil things, Colonel. Am I really forgiven?"

"Yes, you are, Sir. You are forgiven. The shed blood of Jesus has cleansed you from what you did. May I speak over you in prayer?"

He nods.

I pray out in the Spirit in tongues.

Then I speak to the traumatic memory and cast it off him. It flies off and into the covering of the Father over the throne, where it dissolves. This causes the driver to flinch. Knowledge says, "He felt the hit to his power and control."

Meanwhile, the beasts have not moved.

Shama speaks out, "I think they see the covering of the Lord and won't move into it. You know, like the donkey Balaam rode on. Wisdom taught this to us in class from Numbers 22. The spirit realm is real, and sometimes animals see it, even if we don't. We are seeing what Wisdom taught us."

Wisdom says, "Yes, Shama, you are seeing correctly. You have learned this passage. What happened next?"

"Well," she says, "the eyes of Balaam were opened to see the angel of the Lord."

"Great observation," Wisdom replies. "The driver's eyes will be opened to see a blockade in front of them. He won't recognize it as the covering of the Lord because he believes he is in control. He will see it as a separation between the two sitting on the thrones. For him a separation between two authority figures is normal. He will turn the beasts to his right, where the two empty thrones are together. There he will release two of the demonic entities he has in the cart."

Again, I feel Sir quiver. I strengthen my hold on him and continue encouraging him in the spirit.

"Papa," I pray, "please give me understanding on how to help Sir break free from the remaining trauma."

Sir says, "I've seen enough. Can we leave now?"

Wisdom steps in. She looks Sir directly in the eyes. I know She is looking into his spirit. I feel his body start to shake and tremble. This is different from the quivering I felt from him at the presence of evil.

She calls his spirit to the front, "Come forth, spirit of the living God in this man."

The place we are in shakes. I hear a shriek from the darkness behind the thrones.

Knowledge whispers into my spirit, "Her authority," and nods towards Wisdom, "transcends realms and dimensions of realms. They," he points to the darkness, "felt the disturbance as She commanded."

At this point Carmon and Shama's eyes are on Sir, me holding him and Wisdom speaking into his spirit man. I speak out to Carmon, "Focused prayer cover needed here. Ramp it up over Sir in the spirit. Encourage Shama in this also. Sir is close to being totally free. We need him in this fight. We must travail in the spirit. Bless his spirit man to receive what Wisdom is speaking." I feel their intense prayer cover. There is no build up to it; the two of them are tuned in to what's happening with Sir.

My eyes drift to what's happening outside of the covering we are under. It's like everything has been put on pause for what is happening between Sir and the Spirit of Wisdom.

Knowledge speaks into my spirit. "Good call, Colonel. When Wisdom stepped in, Holy Spirit moved into the darkness and used confusion to cause disorientation in the driver's mind. The driver of the cart has stopped moving forward because he's confused about where to go and what he should do. He has completely lost his way."

I glance back to Sir. The covering we are under is intense. There is so much life and power and energy that I feel like I'm going to burst. I see a glow reflect off Carmon and Shama. I realize this must be happening to me also. Carmon nods as she prays in the spirit. The dark cloud of the Lord is now encapsulating the covering we have been under. I think of Psalm 18:11.

He made darkness His secret place;
His canopy around Him was dark waters
And thick clouds of the skies.

He has us in His secret place with Himself.

Knowledge speaks into our group and says, "Pray out Psalm 97:10, *'You who love the LORD, hate evil!'*"

I continue. "We love you, Lord. We know Sir loves You."

Carmon next prays with an authority that shakes all of us, "We hate evil. We hate what it has done to Sir. We know You have preserved his soul and set him apart for Your glory."

Then her prayer completes verse 10, *"He preserves the souls of His saints; He delivers them out of the hand of the wicked."*

Shama prays, "Yes, Lord, he is one of Your saints, and we agree with Your purposes for his life. Deliver him out of the hand of the wicked one. We are standing in agreement for this lost sheep to be totally brought back into the fold."

I picture the Good Shepherd, Jesus, in the parable in Luke 15:4-6.

"What man of you, having a hundred sheep, if he loses one of them, does not leave the ninety-nine in the wilderness, and go after the one which is lost until he finds it? And when he has found it, he lays it on his shoulders, rejoicing. And when he comes home, he calls together his friends and neighbors, saying to them, 'Rejoice with me, for I have found my sheep which was lost!'

"We stand in Your authority, Jesus, to totally and completely bring this one in who was lost but is now saved."

"Yes, Father," Carmon says. "We break off any remaining strongholds holding Sir back."

Shama agrees with a nodding head while she prays in her spirit.

Around us the dark cloud churns and rolls into itself. At the same time, His power is setting Sir free. During all this Wisdom's eyes are locked with Sir's. This is a deep Spirit to spirit transforming connection between the two of them. Thunder rolls and lightning flashes inside the dark cloud. Outside the cloud, I hear shrieks coming from the evil darkness.

Understanding says, "What's happening here is affecting the evil darkness out there," as She nods Her head towards the evil behind the thrones. Hell has lost another one. Sir is free. In that darkness, they have felt the loss. They had a lot invested in him, and now their grip is broken. He is free. To simplify things, with the power of Her intensely deep look, Wisdom has confirmed his true identity and who he is in the Lord."

"And who the Lord is in him," Carmon adds. Both Shama and I nod in agreement.

And Understanding says, "Yes, the life you all live is His life in you. The Father will celebrate this in Heaven, and then Holy Spirit will bring the four of you back here to complete the rest of your mission of observing the placement on the thrones. Your work here has weakened the evil that was planned out there."

I see where Carmon gets it from. When She said, "Out there," She pointed over Her shoulder with Her right thumb. I see She is smiling at my thought, but mostly that Sir really knows who he is.

I'm brought back to the still, gray, early breaking morning in my library chair.

"Thank You, Papa, for totally setting Sir free. For setting all who seek You free. When we seek You, You stop everything to run after us. I bless You today, for You are good. Papa, I pray for continued freedom for Sir and all of us. Thank You for making Your Word real to me. Amen."

OUT SCOUTING

Upon waking this morning, I am in a different place, a different realm. I'm in some type of village. Everything is a dark gray, but I can see clearly. This village is in a forest. The houses are made of some type of stacked up materials, but they almost look like stacks of straw. I'm seeing them through the trees in the forest.

The streets or paths between the trees leading to the houses are clean. I see no signs of clutter or trash on the ground. Everything is very clear. I'm in a valley. Looking up to my right, I see the sky is dawning a new day. At least I think it's a new day because of the light in the sky.

Up on the hill to my right through the trees in the forest, I see the thrones. I'm behind them, but not directly behind them. "The position that Carmon said was deep darkness must be beyond this village," I think.

"Yes, it is," a familiar voice next to me says. The voice is Carmon's. She moves next to me on the right and extends her right arm to point with an open hand, "On the other side of that structure is where we felt the deep darkness. I believe it's gray here because of the overshadowing darkness. Up to the right are the thrones. Beyond them is our covered secret place in the Lord. And what are you doing out here by yourself, Colonel?"

"I'm not sure," I answer. "I woke up this morning in this place."

"Where did you go to sleep last night?" she asks.

I think, "This is an odd question."

She says, "No, it's not. A lot of times the Lord will move us in the night from one realm to another."

Speaking back to her spirit to spirit I say, "Our cottage in the woods."

She says, "Ah, yes, another safe place. A place where He projects the spirit realm into your spirit. From there and other safe places, He brings you into the realms. He must be showing you something. He either wants to confirm something we saw or missed, or He wants you to see it, too."

I'm impressed that she would say she might have overlooked something. She is pretty sharp.

"Thanks, Colonel, for thinking that of me, but in the darkness of any realm we can miss things. Sometimes they are so hidden by layers upon layers of darkness they can't be seen easily. One must focus to see past the layers that are hiding something."

I say, "Well, we are here. Let's ask Papa to give us the eyes to see. See if there is something you missed or something I need to confirm."

She says, "Good call, Colonel. I believe we will need extra covering to gain insight."

"Yes, you're right," I respond. "Papa, please provide the covering we need in this place. Also sharpen our vision to see and tune our ears to hear what You want us to see and hear."

I hear Carmon's, "Amen."

When she says "Amen," I feel a presence next to us. "Understanding, is this You?" I ask.

"Yes, it is, Colonel. You are not only seeing clearer but sensing clearer also."

She nods to Carmon, and she nods back and says, "Thanks for coming."

She says, "I'm here at the bidding of the Father. First to let you both know that We and they," She points up past the thrones where the others are in the secret place, "have you covered. The Father also placed a flexible covering over you both while we are here. I can pass through the realms and dimensions of realms unnoticed while on assignment from Him. Yes, Colonel, to answer that thought, like He showed you with the little bird, the goat, and your friend in a dream."

Carmon looks at me in wonder.

Understanding says to her, "Another training class the Colonel was in while he was in a dream state." She nods and She continues, "Let's take a walk through this place. There is more to see here. Since you have asked for sharper vision, let's see what's here."

The flexible covering moves with us as we start to travel. Trees and rocks are no problem for this covering. We pass right through them.

Carmon says, "I love it when we get to do this in the spirit." As she says that, we stop like we hit something.

Understanding says, "We can move forward, but what do you think is stopping us at this point?"

Carmon and I look at each other with questioning eyes. I shrug my shoulders and ask, "Did we come up against something hidden?"

She says, "That's it, Colonel. We ran into something we didn't see before."

"Exactly," Understanding says. "We have moved past the first surface layer and are moving to the next. This layer has covered a hiding place for another team. It's empty at present but will be occupied soon. It's not too different from the place where you were up there." She points to the place in front of the thrones. She continues, "The Father has hidden secret places waiting for teams to fill them. Even in this place of deep darkness, He has hidden places for strike forces to engage from and regroup in. Notice I didn't say places for teams to hide in. These will be units of highly trained individuals who will go in and back out virtually unnoticed, except for the damage done to the evil powers of darkness.

"Metak's father was on one of these teams. In his zeal he stayed alone and exposed too long and got taken out by the darkness he was fighting. It's important that when the Father places someone in a team to fight, they are to fight as a team to avoid a tragedy like this. Metak's father has his place in heaven with the Father, but he got there a little before he needed to." Understanding holds up Her right index finger and says, "Lesson to learn in team training to avoid needless casualties."

I believe She is speaking to us about our involvement in the teams where we are assigned.

"Yes, Colonel, I am. Let's keep moving to see if we bump into something else."

We pass through that secret place, through trees, then one of the stacked homes, and then on to a large rock formation. She stops our movement at the edge of the rock formation.

Carmon says, "Shama and I came past this rock formation and had some evil feelings but kept moving."

I begin to smell a bad smell. It's something I remember from the past when getting close to an enemy stronghold.

She says, "You are both discerning evil, Carmon." She points to her, then to the rock formation. "You felt the evil. Feelings are a good identifier. The next step is to ask, 'Is this residue or occupied?'" Looking at me, "Colonel, you're smelling evil. Is it because it's here now or is it because it was here previously?"

When I look at Carmon, I see she's looking at me, and we both point and whisper, "It's here."

"Yes," She says. "Around the back side is a crevasse where they pass in and out." Pointing back to Carmon, She says, "You identified this place as a place of deep darkness, and you were right. It is. You were unsure of where its stronghold was, but here it is under the layers of this rock formation. This is how we as a team work together. You're seeing," She points to Carmon. "You're smelling," She points to me, "and I," She points to Herself, "am bringing understanding. Wisdom has taught you both to use Us for the Father's glory. This is a lesson on that skill."

We start to move again around the rock formation past the crevasse entrance. The smell is really bad. Carmon covers her nose and nods to me in agreement because I have mine covered, too. We move around to a staging area to see where the cart and beasts originated from. Unlike the village, this place is filthy and smelly.

Understanding says, "To answer thoughts both of you are thinking, no, we are not going in there. I think you are getting a sense of what's in there without the need to go in."

We both nod at Her good idea not to enter the crevasse. Moving past the staging area, we enter another part of the village. This part is also gray and empty. Understanding says, "This was a nice village and will be again. The villagers let darkness in, one small idea at a time, until they were overwhelmed by it and had to either succumb to it or move on. Most learned their lessons and left to find another place. A few stayed and are pawns of the evil here. Like Sir said, at this point, it's easier for them to obey the instructions of evil than to bear the torture of it."

Carmon says what I'm thinking, "Sad state of affairs with this village."

"Yes, it is," Understanding says, "but it's not the end of it."

We continue to move past the stacked homes to another stopping point. This place has nothing around it. It's open. The trees are spaced apart, and it seems peaceful. "Is there a reason we stopped here?" I ask.

Just then it begins to feel like our flexible secret place is resting on the ground.

"Let's take a look," Understanding says. She asks both of us, "What do you see among the trees and open spaces?" Carmon and I focus outside our flexible secret place. There is nothing except trees and open spaces.

Understanding clears Her throat. We look at Her, and She looks down. We look down to see a blond-haired head pop up through a low place under us. Carmon is quick to reach for her sword. I say, "Ollie, what are you doing here?" At my inquiry, Carmon relaxes.

He crawls up into the secret place and says, "Wisdom sent me out to check on you guys. I only have a few minutes and have to get back." He looks at me and says, "Great to see you, Colonel." I give him a side hug and say the same. Looking towards Carmon, he says, "You must be Carmon. Shama has told me about you. Says she has learned a lot from you. Can't wait to hear more."

Carmon nods as her blue eyes connect with his. She is looking deep into his spirit. She says, "Yes, I am. She has told me about you also. She says you two have learned a lot in Wisdom's class and knows you'll do great out here," as she motions with her right arm.

"Thanks for telling me that," he says. He looks around and says, "Wow! Bad smell out here."

"Yes," I respond, "it's the smell of evil with the mixture of wild beasts."

His eyes scan the scene, taking it all in. He asks, "Well, what is there for me to report back?"

Our time with Ollie goes quickly. We give him our reports and findings, and he's back down in the place where he came out.

"That was quick," I say to Understanding. "But Wisdom is with us over there." I point to the secret place out front of the thrones, "What was all that about?"

"Yeah, I was thinking the same," Carmon says, questioning.

Again, Understanding clears Her throat and looks down.

"Are we supposed to follow?" I ask.

She shakes Her head and says, "No, I wanted you to see an access point. There are entrance and exit points in all realms. This is one of them here behind enemy lines. They know they are here but don't know where they are. The Father keeps them hidden, even from Us at times.

"Wisdom wanted to get Ollie out of the classroom. Since Shama has been here with you, Carmon," She nods at her, "he has been a little anxious in class. Wisdom knows what's going on out here, in the secret place in front of the thrones, and back in the classroom."

I nod and smile. I notice Carmon is pondering. I ask, "What's up?" Understanding starts to move us along again.

She looks up and says in a sad tone, "I thought I saw what was here."

Understanding is quick to wrap around her, even before I can move. There is a deep impartation through a few tears shed from Carmon's eyes.

She says to her, "We all are on eternal learning missions. You know this. Let's be thankful the Father sent Me to bring understanding, to give you and the Colonel an expanded vision. You didn't miss anything. There was just more to see."

"Wow," I think, "these seven Spirits know Their identity, Who they are, and what They bring."

Our movement brings us back to the secret place in front of the thrones. Everything is where we left it in the pause. I know there is still more to see out there, but we were shown what we needed to see. Understanding releases Carmon, and we are back in the secret place in front of the thrones with Holy Spirit, Sir, Shama and the rest of the seven.

I'm glad to be back in the secret place with the others. But I'm very thankful for the scouting we did outside of it, for the lessons we were taught, and the intel gained.

"I thank You also, Papa, for the clarity of vision. Where do we go from here?"

OCCUPIED THRONES

It's 5:02 when I wake up. Although it's still dark outside, it seems light. I get up and walk to the library and notice light shining through the blinds. All is quiet and still. In the kitchen I look out the window to see where this light is coming from. An almost full moon in the clear dark sky reflects the light of the sun.

This reminds me of a time when I was driving in the country on a curvy road at night. It was very dark, and I was careful to watch the road. A thought goes through my mind, and I begin to think back on that night from the perspective of being in the spirit. It must have been a thought placed in my mind from Holy Spirit. The thought was, "What do we as Christians look like in the world?" As I had that thought, I came to a curve in the road. In front of me the darkness moved towards me and got brighter. Another car approached with the headlights shining on the road. The headlights lit the path for that car and gave light on my side of the road, too.

The answer in my mind was, "You look like that in the darkness."

The car passed, and the road was dark again except for my headlights. Then another car approached, and the same thing happened again.

Anyone who drives is probably thinking, "Pretty basic common sense." Yes, that's true, but this was how the Lord answered the question. I realized He spoke to me out of an everyday occurrence, and I got excited about that. I wasn't in a prayer meeting or an intense worship service. I was alone in my car on a dark country road.

Next, He asked, "You want to see what of group of Christians looks like in the world?" I didn't even have time to answer before three or four cars following each other came around the next curve. I have never forgotten this simple analogy the Lord showed me that night.

As I ponder that memory, the moon light shines through the blinds of the library windows and takes me back to the warfare realm. Even in this dark place, the light of the moon shines through the darkness.

Holy Spirit is there in the secret place. He says, "The light of anyone who believes will always overpower even the darkest of nights. This is why when you are on an assignment, We cover you. The dark cloud of the Father is a living dark cloud to those in Him, and a dark thick cloud like an impenetrable wall to those opposing Him." A scripture comes to mind:

> Now thanks be to God who always leads us in triumph in Christ, and through us diffuses the fragrance of His knowledge in every place. For we are to God the fragrance of Christ among those who are being saved and among those who are perishing. To the one we are the aroma of death leading to death, and to the other the aroma of life leading to life. And who is sufficient for these things? For we are not, as so many, peddling the word of God; but as of sincerity, but as from God, we speak in the sight of God in Christ. (2 Cor. 2:14-17)

Holy Spirit continues, "Yes, in Him you are the aroma of Christ everywhere you go. The aroma of Christ emanates from you just like His light."

Our conversation is interrupted by a voice speaking next to me. Holy Spirit defers to Sir as he speaks. I turn in the direction of Sir with a smile on my face.

He asks, "Getting another upload, Colonel?"

"Yes," I respond. "Holy Spirit brought back a memory of an on-the-road training lesson. It's about who we are in Christ. Speaking of who we are in Christ, there seems to be a brighter light about you. How you doing?"

"Colonel," he says, "I am a new creation in Christ. It's one thing to know your past sins are forgiven, but it's another to believe they are. I've heard it said our memories are like an onion. When we peel them back, it may bring tears, but a cleansing comes through tears."

"That's very good, Sir," I reply. "Whenever a memory is brought up, sometimes it's a good one, like I just had from Him. At other times, not so good." I nod to him, "Like you just mentioned, we must realize He is the One bringing them up for His greater good in and through us. In this secret place with Him and others, like the ones here," I glance around, "it's a safe place for Him to work His good pleasure in our lives."

Shama has been standing by our side listening to our conversation. "Colonel, may I speak?" she asks.

"By all means. What's on your mind?"

"Is it okay for His good pleasure to make us happy also?"

I look at Sir and say, "That might be a better question for Sir," as I smile at him.

Sir answers her question, and it sounds like he's being directed by the Spirit of Counsel.

"Shama," he says, "I'm realizing in all things He is good," as he points up. "And the overflow of His goodness gives us," he puts his hands on his chest, "a happiness that is beyond what the world gives us. His pleasure is expressed in the joy He gives us, which we feel as happiness. This is the kind of happiness or joy the world can't give us. And if the world can't give it to us, then the world can't take it away from us."

Sir speaks out of the newly felt joy in his own life.

Shama says, "Like that scripture where it says about Jesus, you know, 'For the joy set before Him, He endured the cross.'"

Sir defers to the Spirit of Understanding who says, "Yes, Shama, but let's look a little deeper into that passage in Hebrews 12:1-2.

> *"Therefore we also, since we are surrounded by so great a cloud of witnesses, let us lay aside every weight, and the sin which so easily ensnares us, and let us run with endurance the race that is set before us, looking unto Jesus, the author and finisher of our faith, who for the joy that was set before Him endured the cross, despising the shame, and has sat down at the right hand of the throne of God."*

I think, "It's interesting that there is a throne mentioned in this verse, not just any throne, but the throne of God."

Understanding continues, "The Cross gave access to all who come to Jesus to also have access to the Father. The great cloud of witnesses surrounds you, and they are filled with joy. The great cloud of witnesses increases your joy, and you increase theirs. Everyone who comes to Jesus experiences the compounded feeling of joy. This does so much more than make you happy. So, yes, when one feels His good pleasure, happiness is a byproduct."

Shama nods her head, smiles, and says, "Good. I just wanted to make sure I can be happy, even when we are in a place like this," as she points past the thrones towards the deep darkness.

Understanding says, "Especially in a place like this. It's not only good, but important to tap into His good pleasure and feel His joy. That's exactly what Jesus did when He was in the dark place. As a matter of fact, He took on all that darkness for you and Sir," as She nods at him, "to be free from it, even while you are in it."

Carmon breaks into the conversation, "Speaking of deep darkness, the cart is on the move again. Holy Spirit has lifted the pause. Let's see what the driver is bringing."

Just as we were told, the driver turns to his right, towards the two empty thrones on the end. There are sounds of shrieks and a rustling in the background.

"Darkness makes its own disturbance in the atmosphere," Understanding says.

As the cart approaches from behind, the person on the third throne is uneasy about the approaching darkness and evil.

We can hear his thoughts, "Whatever is approaching must realize I'm sitting here, and the authority I have can't be touched."

"He's in for a surprise," Sir says. "I've seen this happen in the past. He won't be able to withstand that much of evil for long." Sir shakes his head. "He won't be able to handle it by himself. He needs the Lord."

We all nod in agreement as we continue to observe. "Prayer cover," I speak out, "Even though he's not a believer, we need to cover him in prayer." The others start to pray in the spirit as we observe. Even through the evil presence, we can see the countenance of the person on the throne yield to our prayers. This is a lesson for all of us about how we should cover those sitting in authority.

"Good observation, Colonel," I hear from Counsel.

I nod in appreciation, continue to pray, and observe. The cart moves around to the end throne and stops.

A demonic entity stands in the cart and moves to the side to get off. We hear the sound of an impact hit our secret place, but nothing moves. The demonic entity must have heard it also, as it and the driver are staring in our direction. My heart pounds faster.

Knowledge speaks into our spirits, "They can't see us. They wonder what repelled their power and didn't simply receive their stolen authority. No worries. They will discard it as an anomaly in the spirit."

The entity then jumps off the cart and stands on the throne.

"This is my throne," it says. "I control this throne and everything around it." Then it sits down.

The person on the throne nearest to the entity slides as far as he can in his throne to get away from the usurper. The other person, two thrones down the line, just snickers like he is still in charge.

Knowledge speaks into our spirits, "What did that entity say?"

Shama says, "It said, 'I'm in control.'"

"Good," he says, "So what does that tell you?"

Carmon responds, "It told us who it is. It must be the spirit of control."

"Yes, it is," Sir responds as he nods his head. He just stands and looks and says nothing else about control.

"These are good observations," Knowledge says. "Let's continue to observe."

The cart moves again to the next empty throne. The person on the third throne from our left puffs himself up to look bigger. The next entity stands. Again, we feel a disturbance hit our secret place. Both entities and the driver look our way. I see a flash of red in their eyes.

Sir winces a bit but says, "They can't see us. We are covered. If they could see us, we would feel it. I still feel the Father's pleasure. That's how I know they can't see us."

The second entity steps down from the cart and walks around a bit. It looks at the empty throne. Then it looks at the person on the third throne and at the other entity.

He says to the other entity, "You may have control, but I get into people's minds. I bring confusion and doubt." It looks at the person on the third throne and snarls. That person is looking the other way, one leg crossed over the other with his right hand trying to shield his eyes. Then the entity takes the throne positioned second from our left.

Carmon says, "That one is doubt and confusion."

Knowledge says, "Yes, it is. It will take work to bring accurate knowledge into the affected minds. You can see how to pray and how to use Us to free all those whose minds are confused." Then He turns to us and says, "Also keep yourselves and each other covered in prayer. And most importantly, keep open communication. That entity likes to work on lone rangers."

The cart is on the move again. It passes the third throne and the uncomfortable man sitting on it. The beasts see the anointed throne and pause slightly. The driver only sees the barricade of separation between the two thrones. A crack of the whip, and the beasts continue.

Sir doesn't flinch. His focus is resolute. As the cart passes the other occupied throne, we see the person is still puffed up in pride. The driver eyes the person, but the person doesn't make eye contact. I think, "That's a hit to his pride. He wouldn't look the driver in the eye. How's he going to lead?"

"Another good observation, Colonel," I hear in my spirit from Understanding.

I respond with a nod and thanks.

The cart stops at the last throne. The driver turns and says roughly to the last entity, "Time for you to get off."

The entity responds, "Oh, are we here already? Can't we just drive around a bit more?"

The driver raises his whip at this entity, who responds, "Alright, already! Let me get my stuff." The entity gathers up its stuff while the driver raises the whip again. It says, "I'm coming. Don't be in such a rush. What else do you have to do except get those stinking beasts back to their crib?"

The driver shakes its head as its red eyes glare impatiently at the last entity. Slowly and passively, the last entity heads for the throne. It mumbles, "Oh, I wonder how long I have to sit here doing nothing?" The whip cracks, and the beasts shake their heads, flinging drool onto the entity.

As it wipes off the drool, it says, "I hate those filthy beasts. Not good for much but trudging around." It walks up to the throne and says, "Well, I guess this is it. This is my big assignment. I wish it were already over. Whatever happens, happens. I'll just go with it." It climbs up into the last throne and gets situated.

The cart is gone, whips cracking as it disappears into the darkness.

Knowledge speaks into our spirits, "What do you think this entity represents?" It's quiet in the secret place.

I say, "It seems complacent."

Carmon says, "Yeah, real passive."

Sir says, "Must be complacency or passivity?"

Shama has her hand on her chin like she's thinking, but she doesn't speak.

Understanding speaks into our thoughts, "Yes, this is the spirit of passivity. It doesn't care about anything, and whatever happens, happens," as She shrugs Her shoulders with Her hands palms up.

Wisdom enters the spirit conversation, "Five of the six thrones have been occupied. Metak will be taking his place among them at the appointed time. For now, you will be receiving further training for engagement in this realm. Sir, you and Shama will be heading back to the classroom to add to the report."

Sir raises his hand. "Yes," She says to him.

"You said add to the report. Has a report been turned in?"

I look at Carmon, and she at me. Then we both look at Wisdom.

Wisdom responds, "We have a partial report from a field agent who was sent to spy out the land. We will cover that with the rest of the team in the classroom."

Sir nods in affirmation. At his nod, he and Shama disappear from our sight.

Wisdom turns to Carmon and me. She says, "You two have been through previous battles in the past. The team will depend on you for input and support. This usually is the hardest part for seasoned warriors. You are to train and assist. For the most part, they will engage. There may be times when all hands and experience are needed. Then through Our guidance," as She waves her hands at the Seven, "You will assist in that." For now, She nods towards Carmon, "You will be heading back to your advanced class."

Carmon snaps to attention, salutes from the heart, nods, and says, "Colonel."

I return the salute, and she bows from the waist towards Wisdom, as one would bow towards royalty. Wisdom nods. When Carmon arises from her bow, she disappears from my sight. I turn towards the Seven and bow the same as Carmon. When I arise from the bow, I find myself back in a chair. In the natural, I have also been walking through my day. This chair is in a waiting room at an outpatient clinic. I am along as support.

I find it interesting the Seven left me in this place.

Holy Spirit says, "They are here just as We are, hidden in plain sight. Training will resume as usual, here a little, there a little. Be attentive."

A breeze blows over me as I continue to wait in the waiting room.

"I bless You, Papa, and thank You for this day. Help me to be aware of Your closeness as I go through it. Amen."

KINGDOM FOCUS

Upon awakening I see a bright orange haze under a cloud-covered sky. I realize I'm in another realm. I get up and head to my chair in our cottage library.

In the library, I focus and move back into the spirit realm. The bright orange haze comes from flames below the haze in the sky. Everything around the haze and the flames is pitch black. The sounds of faint but distinct screams and shrieks add to the sight of the flames in the orange sky. The sounds cause me to stand perfectly still, mostly because the intensity of these sights and sounds have glued my feet to the ground like I'm in concrete.

My heart rate increases. My skin begins to get cold and clammy. I look at my feet, but they aren't in concrete. They are not even on the ground. I'm in a weightless state, floating above the ground. In this weightless state, I wonder about all this and ask, "Papa, where am I, and what's happening in front of me?"

I hear, "No worries, child. You are just passing by."

The sound of the voice and the way it speaks feel comforting, but different. I can't tell if it's male or female. It comes from outside and inside at the same time. The voice is peaceful and calming. The phrase, "No worries, child." is new to me. I know I'm a grown man, and I know I'm a child of God.

I hear the voice again, "Gehenna. You are passing by Gehenna."

Hearing this causes my skin to chill. More screams and shrieks increase the chill. Fear doesn't enter my being, but I feel uneasy. I want to look, but I don't want to look, so I don't look. I pray, "Papa, what do I focus on? Why am I seeing and hearing this?"

Again, the soothing voice says, "No worries, child. You are just passing by. You don't have to look to know what is happening. Your focus is to remain on the Father. You are covered by the life-giving blood of Jesus."

Hearing this, I close my eyes to focus on the Father. The orange haze and brightness of the flames are being overshadowed by a bright, glowing light. The screams and shrieks are replaced with singing and joyful praises.

I may be passing by Gehenna, but my spirit does not detect its sights or sounds. Neither are they felt in my being as I focus on the Father. My skin and heart rate are both normal. All I feel in this weightless state of wonder is the anticipation of seeing the Father. The stillness and quiet carry me to another place above the flames of Gehenna.

I hear, "Yes, a place in the Father you have not been before. A place of peace in the storm. A place of comfort and security amidst the chaos of the world around you. Your spirit is in the hands and realm of the Father. The One Who is, Who was, and Who is to come."

I ask, "Papa, who is the voice speaking to me?"

I hear, "Does it really matter, My child? I cause the voice to speak to you. I move you from one realm to the next. I move you from earth, through the second heaven, to the third heaven of My dwelling."

As He answers, I know this is Papa speaking to me. "I give You praise for taking me past Gehenna and into Your glorious presence. I bless You today, Papa. You are holy." The words of Matthew 6:6 well up in my spirit:

> But you, when you pray, go into your room, and when you have shut your door, pray to your Father who is in the secret place; and your Father who sees in secret will reward you openly.

And then onto verses 6:9-10:

> *In this manner, therefore, pray:*
> *Our Father in heaven,*
> *Hallowed be Your name.*
> *Your kingdom come.*
> *Your will be done*
> *On earth as it is in heaven.*

His voice speaks again, "For My will to be done on earth as it is in heaven, My people need to come for a visit, so they can bring it back with them. Too many of My children are living close to Gehenna. They are living so close, it's all they can see. For My kingdom to be established on earth, the focus needs to change from earth to heaven.

"The constant gaze of Jesus My Son was always on Me in heaven. Did He see evil when He was on earth? Yes. Did He see people hurting and in trouble? Yes. Was His gaze and His focus on what He saw in the natural? No. It was on Me and My answer to the evil and the hurt and the pain and the shame. He was only able to bring heaven to earth when He stayed focused on Me.

Heaven is in Me. Heaven comes out of Me. He even brought heaven to Gehenna to make the way for heaven to come to earth. Because of His constant focus on Me, a way was made for My will, which is done in heaven, to be done in earth. No worries, My child. You are just passing by, not through. My Son passed through so you and all others could pass by or bypass hell on your way to heaven.

"To answer your prayer, 'Come, Thy kingdom, be done in and on earth, as it is in heaven.' The first step is to come. Come to Me. Come to the heavenly realms, which are Me. When you come to Me, I can give you what's needed in and on earth. My Son came from heaven to earth to establish a way from earth to heaven so that My heaven has a way to earth through My people."

The only words that come from my spirit are, "Holy. Holy. Holy. You are holy. I join with the angels and cry holy. Isaiah 6:1-3 pulses through me.

In the year that King Uzziah died, I saw the Lord sitting on a throne, high and lifted up, and the train of His robe filled the temple. Above it stood seraphim; each one had six wings: with two he covered his face, with two he covered his feet, and with two he flew. And one cried to another and said:

> *"Holy, holy, holy is the LORD of hosts;*
> *The whole earth is full of His glory!"*

"Let this be, Papa. You are holy. You are holy. You are holy. The whole earth is filled with Your glory.

"Papa, help us to see heaven so we can bring it back to earth. Open our eyes to see Your kingdom being established on and in earth as it is in Heaven."

THE GUARDS

It's 5:55 a.m., and I'm in my library chair in our cottage in the woods. It was a busy day yesterday, and I woke from a full night's sleep to a figure standing in front of me in the spirit. The figure is a big, ugly-looking, very strong man with a heavy chain around his neck.

He doesn't look pleasant. The big chain is wrapped twice around his neck and lays over his right shoulder. It is attached to a looped holder in the ground. Past him are two covered graves and another similar-looking big man beyond the graves. I see the second man from the back, and he, too, has a chain wrapped twice around his neck and over his right shoulder and attached to a loop in the ground. The backs of both men are towards the covered graves. Both are dressed in a piece of gray cloth, covering short pants.

I'm in the cemetery, and I believe I'm here to speak to the two graves between the men. As I start to pray in my spirit, I'm surrounded by the presence of Holy Spirit. His presence covers me and separates me from the feeling of demonic power emanating from these two men. A question is in my mind, "I believe I'm here to do battle?" At that thought, from a distance in the natural, I hear an owl hooting outside our cottage. Wisdom is near, and I feel I must address Her and call forth Her presence. As I pray more intensely in tongues, I feel an increase of the Spirit of the Lord around me.

Thankfulness wells up from deep within my spirit. "I thank You, Papa, for sending Your presence. I come to You in the Spirit of the Lord that rests upon Your Son Jesus Who lives in me. I thank You for coming, Spirit of the living, eternal God. Help me to partner with You today and with the seven Spirits Who are present with You. I invite You, Spirit of Wisdom, to speak into my spirit."

Immediately I feel a rush in my spirit and around me. I feel the covering of the Spirit of Wisdom wrapped around me like a shield of armor. If She is here, the others are also. A shield covers me and brings the presence of a holy fear.

I see the two men through this holy fear, and they are getting anxious. They are pulling at the chains around their necks trying to loosen them, to no avail. The chains are affixed tightly and are not going to be pulled out or broken off them. They feel something coming against their assigned authority to guard the two graves.

The voice of Wisdom speaks into my spirit, "It was a good thing you didn't address the two men guarding the graves. You are not here to battle them."

"I'm not?" I ask. "Actually, I'm glad I'm not, but why am I here, and why are they here?"

Knowledge speaks up and says, "May I ask a question?" Wisdom defers to Knowledge. He nods a thanks to Wisdom, as He steps up to speak with me. He stands between me and the men guarding the graves. A misty presence shields my view of the men and the graves.

Out of this presence Knowledge asks me, "What is your assignment here in this cemetery?"

Thinking for a moment, I feel another presence behind me nudging me to speak. I feel total peace. I realize this is the Spirit of Understanding behind me. She starts massaging my head. I remember the reason I've come to this place. I say to Knowledge, "I'm here to speak to the graves."

He says, "Exactly." Then He asks, "Why do you think you're here to do battle with the guards of these graves?" I look past Him to the men guarding the graves. With a soft touch against the left side of my head, Knowledge turns my head back to face Him and says, "Focus on Me, not them."

I answer, "Well, they are standing in the way of the graves I'm to address."

He says, "They are not your assignment. You are here to speak to the graves."

I respond with, "Yes but . . ." and feel a hand over my mouth. It's Understanding's hand, keeping me from speaking.

Knowledge defers to Wisdom by saying, "You need to take it from here."

She gladly steps in and speaks, "Do you remember chapter 30 and verse 8 in the book of First Samuel where it says, 'So David inquired of the Lord'?"

"Yes, I remember that," I nod and mumble through the covering over my mouth.

"Do you also remember what's in Second Samuel 6:6-7?"

"Yes," I say, "It's when David had a new cart made, and they were bringing the Ark back. Uzzah was killed for steadying the Ark."

"Yes," She says, "David had a good idea but didn't seek the Lord. If he had sought the Lord like he did about the pursuit of the Amalekites, Uzzah would not have died. Too many times there have been and are unnecessary casualties. Your mission in the cemetery is only to speak to the graves and only to speak to them through Us in the reverent fear of the Lord. Battling for the Lord is a team mission. It's a body mission, as it says in Ephesians 4:16:

> from whom the whole body, joined and knit together by
> what every joint supplies, according to the effective working
> by which every part does its share, causes growth of the body
> for the edifying of itself in love.

"The last words of verse 15, just before the statement about body ministry, is 'Christ is the head.'

"Too many times the body has not let Jesus be the head, and therefore the body has not been edified in love with each part doing its share. If one does it all, there is no need for the body. Jesus knew this personally. He pointed the way to the Father and only did His will.

"We have someone else to take care of the guards. You are only to speak to the graves."

I think, "What are they guarding in the graves?"

Knowledge speaks to the question in my mind, "Understanding will come from the Father in His timing. For now, you are to pray for the removal of the guards."

"Isn't this doing battle against the guards?" I ask.

Understanding says, "I'll speak to that. It's my turn to do a little review. Do you remember when you were praying for Sir in the classroom?"

"Yes," I say, "there were three of us and You seven, of course."

"Good," He says, "Did you do the deliverance?"

"No," I respond, "I assisted in prayer."

"Yes, She answers, "all three of you assisted in prayer. Who did you assist with your prayers?"

I think for a few seconds and say, "We assisted You to speak through us. As long as we stayed spirit focused, You all guided us in our prayers, words, and actions. You all worked through us."

"Yes," Understanding answers and continues. "It is no different here. You are to pray as We lead you. Your prayers will empower Us through the Spirit of the Lord, activating the Spirit of Might. Might will then speak or direct the person who is to battle against the guards."

Thinking again for a few seconds, I ask, "What's my first step in this process? Right now it's me, them," as I point towards the guards, "and You seven," waving my hands at Them.

Knowledge steps back in and says, "Let Me ask you a question. You now know two things. You are to speak the graves. The last time you did this, you spoke as We empowered you to speak. Yes?"

"Yes," I respond with a nod.

He continues, "Okay then, you also know you're not to battle them," as He points over His shoulder with His right thumb.

"Yes," I respond with another nod.

Understanding paces by Knowledge's side, as Knowledge says, "I believe Understanding wants to bring understanding." He turns to give Understanding a nod to speak. Understanding is quick to jump in, with a nod to Knowledge.

"Okay, Colonel," She says, "We are at war, and you need assistance. You are in a position of leadership. You are to train and assist."

I feel understanding stirring in my spirit. "Yes," I say, "I see where You're going with this." Understanding stops Her pacing in front of me, and Her glowing presence penetrates my spirit man. With so much life and spiritual activity happening, I'm surprised the guards are not even stirring, except for a tug on the chains every once in a while."

"Oh, they know something is up," Understanding says as Her presence moves to the side so I can see the guards. Their heads are on a swivel, and their eyes are straining to see what's happening. I even see them get a glimpse of each other and hear them growl at each other. "I guess this is their language," I say.

Understanding moves back between me and the guards and says, "No, not their language. They don't like each other. Each is territorial, and each thinks the other is not needed. Now back to our conversation," She says, as She looks into my spirit. She knows my spirit is energized by Her penetrating stare. "Okay. Knowledge got the two reasons out of the way. Now let's get back to the person who is to do battle with the guards. Where is he, Colonel?"

She emphasizes, *Colonel* like She's giving me a hint. I respond with a shrug, look around, and say, "I'm not sure."

"Well, what are you going to do about that, Colonel?"

Again, She emphasizes *Colonel.* I put my right hand on my chin and say, with hesitation, "I guess I need to pray about that."

"Bingo," She says. "You need to pray him in. Ask the Father to stir Us to stir him to get him here to take care of the guards. Then you will be released and guided by Us to speak to the graves."

I feel my spirit welling up in me like a pressure cooker. I burst out in tongues, and the atmosphere shifts. The guards sway in their positions and tug violently at their chains although the chains don't release from where they are anchored. The power of my prayer in the spirit increases, and the ground starts to shake beneath my feet. I'm guided to look to my right. Two people are walking towards the guards. It's a woman and a young boy, holding hands. The boy looks to be maybe 10 years old.

I hear Wisdom say, "Pray for guidance for them to know what to do."

I pray, "Give them understanding for what they need to do, Father. I call for Wisdom to be present with them to speak and act through them with the Spirit of Might."

The shaking under my feet continues, and this gets the attention of the guards. They hold onto their chains to steady themselves. With each step the young boy takes, the ground shakes more. I feel myself being lifted off the ground. Understanding says, "We lifted you up to steady you. Keep praying."

A power of deep intercession overtakes me. I'm lost in the power of prayer as I watch what's happening in front of me. The misty cloud Wisdom, Knowledge, and Understanding have been speaking from expands to encompass the woman and the boy. They continue their slow, steady pace as they approach the guards. The guards are freaking out. They sense a fight is coming.

I hear in my spirit, "Pray through your observation. Pray."

I feel others around me. Sir is standing next to me, along with Shama and Ollie.

Sir says, "We were sent as prayer support with you to cover them." He points towards the woman and the boy walking towards the guards.

I say, "I'm glad you are here."

He says, "Your prayers stirred the Father to bring us to assist."

Ollie says, "Great to be here, Colonel. Who are those big guys? Man! They smell bad."

I think, "I've been involved with this to the point I'm not smelling like I should."

I hear, "Don't think. Continue to pray. We have blocked your sense of smell. Ollie needs to learn what's out there."

I say, "The big, smelly guys are guarding those two graves."

Ollie asks, "Why are they guarding graves? What's in them? Buried treasure?"

I think, "Buried treasure. Maybe he's onto something. What's in those graves must be very valuable to the Father, and the enemy wants to keep it buried."

Again I hear, "Focus. Don't think."

"We'll get to that later, Ollie. We are here to pray for those two," as I point towards the woman and the boy.

Ollie nods.

I mumble a question to myself, "They look familiar. Great authority is walking with them. I wonder who they are?"

Ollie says, "Colonel, I'm surprised you don't recognize Syiya and Metak."

"That's Metak?" I say.

Sir says, "Yes, Colonel, while you have been here in the warfare realm, he has grown. He is maturing quickly. Syiya has become more comfortable with us in the class and has recognized the impartation of the seven Spirits of the Lord with Holy Spirit in the lead."

With this new intel, I say, "Well, guys, I'm glad you're here to assist. Let's hammer this place with prayer and give them the cover they need." The intensity of spirit-led prayer increases to a roar in the spirit. Syiya and Metak both look our way and nod in thanks. They have been made visible to the guards. The guards are uncomfortable as they follow Syiya's and Metak's looks towards us.

Knowledge says, "They are only looking into a misty cloud. They don't see you."

"That's awesome," Shama says. "We are free to pray Holy Spirit-led prayers without their interference."

I see Metak has no weapons, but both of them have gold strapped to their feet. Knowledge speaks into my spirit so only I can hear, "Colonel, if his feet are shod, where are his weapons?"

I say, "His weapons? His weapons must be on the inside, in his spirit."

"Yes, they are," Knowledge responds. "Now pray into the activation of what he is to use."

I speak out to the group, "Let's pray into what Metak needs. Pray the Spirit of Wisdom will direct him to use the right weapons to battle the guards."

As we begin deep intercession over Syiya and Metak, I recognize the peace covering them. I also sense boldness rising.

I hear in my spirit, "You and the team pray it out."

I say to the team, "Pray into boldness. Boldness over Metak as they continue to move into position." The team prays.

Shama speaks out first with, "Boldness! Father, release boldness through the Spirit of Might through Metak, as he speaks Your words."

Ollie joins in with, "Yes, Spirit of Might, have Your way through him. Use him mightily in this battle, Father."

"Come, Spirit of Wisdom," Sir prays out. "Lead him in the way he should go. Cover him to say and proclaim only what he needs to say."

I pray out, "I'm in agreement with all your prayers over Metak and Syiya. I send forth Your peace to give them a clear path in the battle."

We all settle in to pray quietly in the spirit as we see Syiya and Metak stop a few steps from the guards. They look very small next to these big, ugly, smelly guards.

The guards snarl and growl out obscenities at them.

I say to the team, "Ramp up the coverage. No curse can alight. Pray. Pray in the Spirit; pray in tongues. Covering prayers need to go out." Another roar of prayers goes out over them. I see a wave of prayer leave us and cover them. The wave hits the guards as it covers Syiya and Metak. The guards are almost knocked over. They stay on their feet by holding onto their chains. Now the guards really know they are up against something bigger than the woman and the boy standing near them.

Syiya turns towards Metak and gets on one knee. Hands on his shoulders, she looks into his eyes. Her mouth is moving, but we don't hear her words to him. I can only imagine she is recounting what Moses said to Joshua, "Be strong and courageous."

Sir says, "I'd bet she's praying for him."

Knowledge speaks through our prayers and comments and says, "Oh, she is saying and doing more than that. She is encouraging him because he is not alone in this fight. He is covered by all your prayers. Wisdom is guiding him, and Understanding and I are with him. The Spirit of Might is his rear guard, and the Fear of the Lord already has the guards shaken."

Syiya stands and steps back. She points to Metak, but we still can't hear her words.

I speak out to the team, "Pray that he hears the instruction of his mother." Another roar of prayer in tongues goes out and covers them, hitting the guards again as they look towards us, only to see the misty presence.

Syiya points to the hooks in the ground where the chains are attached. Metak nods, and Syiya steps back several steps. I have a heightened sense of expectation in my heart, and I know this is true for the team, too. I see Ollie shadow boxing as he's watching and praying. Shama is wide eyed. Her lips are moving in prayer to the words in her spirit. Sir stands confidently, knowing the Fear of the Lord prevails over all of this.

Me? I'm glad to be where I am with this incredible team. I'm also praying for Metak's courage and boldness to continue to move him in this battle with two men who are more than twice his size.

Metak boldly approaches the two giant men. He points to them and boldly speaks out as he points up, "You will not hold back any longer what the Lord God Almighty wants to release from those graves. Your time is up. Your mission is finished, and you will no longer stand in the way of almighty God."

Knowledge speaks into our team, "Agree in prayer with his proclamations against the guards."

The team speaks out in prayer. We are all praying at the same time. I know the seven Spirits hear and are moved. We see another wave going out from us, and the guards shake again.

I almost can't believe what I see Metak do next.

Shama says, "Oh no."

Ollie says, "Metak, what are you doing?"

Sir says, "Atta boy, use them to your advantage."

Understanding speaks into our comments, "Get in agreement here with Sir on this one. He's been here before. He knows what's going to happen."

"Yes, Lord," I pray out, "help us be in agreement about the guidance You're giving Metak."

Ollie and Shama stand in agreement also. I glance towards Syiya to see she is nodding at Metak's actions. Metak is on one knee at the hook in the ground of the first man's chain. Somehow, he easily unhooks the chain. Even the huge man is dumbfounded and doesn't move.

"Pray out!" I command the team. "Pray out for the Spirit of the Lord to hold that man still." We all pray out in agreement.

Next, slow motion takes over in front of us. Metak stands, holding the chain in his left hand like it's weightless. He steps over the graves to the other man. He gets on one knee, and while holding one chain in his left hand, he easily unhooks the other one with his right hand. Then he stands with one chain in each hand. He holds them both up as if weightless and shakes them in the faces of the two men who stand motionless in front of him.

Then he pulls them down with a tug and spins the men around to face each other. He looks at them both and says, "You wanted to be loosed from your bonds. You're loosed. Have at it!" Metak throws the chains on the ground in front of them. Their heads jerk, and he steps back.

The two giants snarl at each other, and they each grab their chains. I can almost hear their grip tighten on the chains. The two men begin to battle with each other. They thrash each other with their chains. The dirt on the graves flies in the air as they scuffle.

A glimmer of gold comes out of one of the graves.

213

Ollie says, "Look! Treasure is under their feet."

The two men draw blood from each other as the battle ensues. They are thrashing and beating each other to a pulp. Their energy quickly dissipates as one falls to his death, and the other can only stagger. He looks towards Metak, who is standing in total peace. The giant man tries to take a step towards him but trips and falls dead, face first on top of the other man. We all are quiet.

Knowledge speaks, "Seal this in prayer. The battle isn't over till it is sealed, not by their blood," as he points to the two giants laying there. "It's sealed by the blood of the Lamb."

Sir prays out, "We thank You, Father, for the victory in this battle. We give You the glory. We thank You for the blood of Jesus that seals this victory."

I add to his prayer, "And we seal this here and now. The victory is Yours."

Shama and Ollie add their amens to this sealing prayer. At their amens the two giants turn to dust and dissolve in front of us. All that's left is a blood stain on the ground.

Syiya gives Metak a hug. They both turn to us and salute from their hearts. We all return the salutes. Sir, Shama, and Ollie disappear from my sight. Syiya and Metak bow at their waists to the seven Spirits of the Lord. The seven Spirits nod in return.

Metak looks at me and points with an open right hand to the partially uncovered graves and then points to me with the same hand. I hear him speak spirit to spirit, "Thanks for the prayer cover. You're up next. The graves are ready for you to speak to them."

I nod to him, and he and Syiya disappear. I turn to the Seven and bow to them. Upon rising, I'm back in my chair in the living room.

The battle to remove the guards took two days in the spirit. I'll be back to speak to the graves in His timing.

"Let it be, Papa. Let it be. Prepare me to receive from You the words to speak to the two graves to release the buried treasure for Your glory. Amen."

WHAT'S IN THOSE GRAVES?

I'm seated in my library chair this morning and feel a rumbling. The chair shakes. My body shakes. With a deep breath, I speak to my spirit, "Peace, be still." Immediately, I'm transported in the spirit to the cemetery where the two guards were fighting over the two graves in front of me. The blood-stained earth is off to the right on the other side of the graves. There is no foul order. There is no evidence the guards were there except for the blood stain.

A slight breeze begins, and dust from the stirred-up mounds on the graves blows over the blood stain and covers it. Soon this too is gone.

I look around and see no one. It's just me, a slight breeze, which I believe is Holy Spirit, and the partially mounded-up graves.

It seems a long time since I've been here, but I know it was just yesterday. I ponder everything that occurred, and I think, "Man! Metak has grown. The incredible authority and boldness he walks in and the presence of peace he carries! When he unhooked those chains, I thought for a minute he might be a goner, but he definitely had the plan of the Father and went with it. Sir has grown, too. I see and hear him stepping into more discernment and authority.

"Okay, Papa. You have me here standing in front of these two graves again. Ollie mentioned something that got me thinking. What do these two graves contain? What could have so much value the evil one put guards over them?"

A misty cloud descends around me. My spirit man fills with excitement at Their presence around me. My whole being is jumping up and down inside me. I almost can't contain myself with the anticipation of what's next. I know in the natural I have a smile from ear to ear.

"Thank You, Father, for sending the Spirits of the Lord again to guide me in how You want me to go and what You want me to do. As I humbly come before You, I know the shed blood of Jesus gives me access. Please tune my ears to hear and sharpen my eyes to see. My spirit man is out front to receive from You, Holy Spirit, and the seven Spirits. I quietly wait in an attitude of praise for You to speak."

While I praise Him, I feel a nudge on my left shoulder and turn to see the Spirit of Knowledge with a smile on His face. I smile and ask, "What's up?"

He points to the graves. I follow His right arm to see the shimmering gold light from one of the graves. The light gets brighter. I ask, "Am I to speak to the graves or just stand and observe?"

I feel a nudge on my right shoulder, and I look to see Understanding with a smile on Her face also. She points to the graves. I follow Her right arm to see a similar brightness from the other grave. Again, I ask, "Am I to speak to the graves or just stand and observe?"

I feel a tap on my head. When I look up, it's the Spirit of Wisdom above me. She is smiling, too. She says, "It's not what's in the graves. It's who!"

"Who?" I ask.

"Yes, who," She says.

I respond, "So the guards were keeping someone in the graves. Not a teaching or a doctrine the Father wants to raise up?"

"That's correct," She says.

I say, "I know Jesus sent out His disciples and gave them power to heal the sick and raise the dead, so it must be Him working through me to do this." To me this seems like a holy thing.

I ask, "Who does He want raised?" With a grin, Knowledge speaks up, "That would be," He pauses and points to Understanding and then back to himself.

I'm thinking, "Okay. He is speaking in some code here. Papa, I come to You in the reverent fear of Who You are. Can You please give me an understanding of this?"

Understanding clears Her throat and says, "Uh, Me and Him," as She points to Knowledge.

I say, "Wait a minute. You two are directing me by the Spirit of the Lord to raise You two from the graves?"

They both smile from ear to ear, nodding. Their heads look like the little bobble head figures on a car's dashboard.

I say, "You're right here next to me," as I look from one to the other. "How can You be in the graves?"

Wisdom interrupts my questioning. She says, "This one's on Me. Your world is not this world. But what and who is in a grave and what and who's released from a grave in this world affects your world. Yes, Knowledge and Understanding are by your side. You see them because the Father has opened your eyes to see them. But true godly knowledge and understanding," she points to the graves, "have been buried by the doctrines of man. Man values worldly wisdom, not wisdom from the Father."

She nods to Knowledge and Understanding, "Worldly knowledge and understanding have replaced them. Both lack true knowledge and understanding. Think about it. Where else can you gain knowledge about something and still be confused? Or gain understanding and still feel like you don't understand. Worldly concepts will always be lacking and only partially understood, even by the propagators of false doctrine."

She points again with an outstretched misty form of a right arm and open hand to the graves. "So, what's lying in those graves was guarded by the evil one because he knows when godly knowledge and understanding are released, he will be seen for the fool he is. We don't have much time. When the enemy realizes his guards are gone, he will replace them, just as he has in the past."

I ask, "They were removed before?"

Wisdom replies, "Oh, yes. They have been taken out several times in the past by lone rangers who didn't have a team to continue to the completion of the mission. The mission is to release Them into Their full potential."

Immediately, I feel to move into a reverent, holy-fear-of-God prayer. I start to pray out in tongues to clear my mind. As I pray, I see dust rolling my way in the distance.

Wisdom says, "It's the storm of the evil one. He's angry. Hurry, son of man! Go deeper into the Spirit of Jesus Who resides in you. Release the authority and power that raised Jesus from the dead and took out hell and the grave."

I look to Knowledge and Understanding. Now their faces look serious and determined. Understanding rubs my shoulders like a trainer with a prizefighter in a ring.

Knowledge speaks into my spirit, "You got this. The eternal power of Jesus lives in you. Speak to that authority. Call it forth."

The tongues rise from deep within me to a roar I have not experienced before. I speak out of the misty presence around me. The English words echo through this realm from inside the mist where I stand with the Seven. Then, the words issue out in another language.

Wisdom says, "Your words are mixed with Spirit power from us, a power the demonic understands."

My words roll like thunder, "Spirit of the living God Who lives in me, come forth in this matter. I stand on the authority of Jesus Christ, the risen Son of the living God. Come wind of the Spirit and blow the remaining dust and dirt from the graves."

A slight breeze starts to flow over my shoulders through Understanding. The breeze is a deep blue, rolling billow. It comes from the Spirit of the Lord and starts to raise the dust off the graves.

I hear shrieks in the distance.

Knowledge encourages, "Go deep, son of man. Go deep. You got this." Understanding rubs my arms like I'm getting ready for the one-two punch.

Wisdom speaks from above, "You can do better than that." She commands my spirit man to come front and center. She says, "Align with the Spirit of the Fear of the Lord."

I feel my spirit become bigger within me and see the shining glory of the Farther emanating from my spirit. I am picked up. Whooooa! This is beyond me. I speak to what's happening. "Rise up, Spirit of the Lord. Have Your way, Spirit of the Fear of the Lord. I speak Your holy, righteous fear over these graves."

The rolling cloud continues towards the graves and me. I see demonic entities with their hands over their ears. Fear covers their beings. They can't escape from the rolling cloud of the Lord.

Another wave of Fear of the Lord tongues rises up, and I release it from within the mist. Chunks of impacted dirt let loose from the graves, and the light shines brighter. The light exposes the fear on the demonic entities as they cover their faces to shield the light, only to get hit by the chunks of impacted dirt flying at them. The flying chunks of dirt impact the rolling cloud like cannonballs, damaging and creating holes in the cloud. Next, I feel someone standing next to me.

I hear a soothing voice, "Colonel, we were sent as backup in this one. Looks like you're doing real good. How can we help?"

I'm overwhelmed by the peace I hear amid this fierce scene. The voice I hear is Sir's, and when I turn to look at him, I also see the faces of those from the class.

Wisdom says, "You're not seeing things. You are experiencing the combined unity in the body of believers. As one speaks guided by Us, they all speak in unity."

"Wow!" I think.

I hear, "Don't think. Speak."

I say to Sir, "Speak out to the wind of the Spirit of the Lord. Your spoken words will empower the wind."

Sir's face doesn't even change. His voice comes as effortlessly as singers go deep within themselves to release the words naturally.

As I hear his voice speaking to the wind, I see his voice come forth like mighty, rushing waters. The words have the collective power of Niagara Falls. The authority of unity, joined with my words, blows the remaining dirt from the graves. Just in time, the remains of dirt whirl against the approaching rolling cloud. I hear blood-curdling screams and shrieks, muffled by the intense sound of the dirt coming off the graves. The rolling cloud is gone. All is quiet.

I hear from Sir, "Wow! That was invigorating."

I look at him/them, and all I see are smiling faces that soon fade from my sight. In front of me are two glowing outlined figures of golden light. Knowledge and Understanding have been standing by my sides, and now, they are moving into their rightful spirit bodies. Tears flow from my eyes like a river. It all happened so fast. "What happened?" I think. "How do I wrap my arms around this?"

Wisdom from above says, "First, receive a hug from Them," as she nods, "They will bring knowledge and understanding."

I look to where She is looking to see the golden glowing figures of the Spirit of Knowledge and the Spirit of Understanding floating towards me. "The graves," I think. "What graves?" There is nothing behind them as they approach. Their arms extended in unity wrap around me. The impartation of Their touch infuses and melts me as one with Them. A knowing quickens the mind of my spirit to receive understanding from a different perspective.

I hear from Them in unison, "You are one with the Father. We are one with the Father. You are one with Jesus. We are one with Jesus. We are all one with His Spirit, Who is Holy."

Wisdom from above descends into the unity of the misty cloud covering me. She doesn't say a word. I know we are one in the Spirit of the Lord. I rest in this oneness.

I'm unsure how long we spent in the oneness of this misty presence or if it even has subsided. But the feel of the leather chair under me in the living room of our home in Moravian Falls brings me back into the natural.

As I ponder this, I think, "Holy Spirit has been speaking to me and teaching me about the authority of my spoken words. Being taught about it and seeing it are two different things. When I stay in and on my assignment, other things get handled. I spoke to the graves, and the rolling evil cloud was removed. Also, I see where adding the combined unity of the believers into the mix of the fight multiplies the power of that authority.

"Wow, where are we going from here?"

"Thank You, Papa. Amen."

WALKING A GRAVEL PATH

I sit with eyes closed on a porch chair on the deck of our Moravian Falls home. The sound of rain hitting the metal roof brings me to a different place, a different realm.

I'm walking a gravel path, and a misty cloud covers me.

On my left, through the mist, the sky is bright and blue. On my right it's dark and very overcast. Up the path on my left are very big, heavy stone columns. Getting closer, I see strong iron sections of fence between the columns. The iron itself seems to gleam, like there is life in it. Trees and shrubs and many-colored flowers are on the other side of the fence.

Then I see the mounds of grave sites situated throughout the trees and shrubs and flowers. This is a cemetery of some sort that is different from the other one I've been in a few times.

I hear in my spirit, "This is a place of remembrance. Yes, there are graves here, but these graves are holding only the bones of the saints who have preceded you."

I ask, "Spirit of Understanding, are we in the warfare realm?"

She replies, "Your senses have been heightened, and you didn't need to ask Who I was."

I respond with, "In the natural I did feel a little different this morning when I woke up. My perspective seems to be clearer."

She says, "Yes, your spiritual sight has been sharpened. How about your hearing? Tell Me what you hear."

Listening, I hear the sound of the atmosphere around me. Whoa, it's like I can hear the air. A light, constant flowing, whirling sound is around me. I almost didn't notice it because of the beautiful sounds of the singing birds.

She says, "Good, good. What else do you hear?"

I stop on the path to eliminate the sound of gravel crunching under my feet. Standing still, closing my eyes, I feel the sounds penetrating my being. I feel the sound of the air going into me and through me. The song of the birds singing bounces through my spirit and being like a majestic concert being performed around me. Then I hear voices. At least I think they are voices.

I hear, "Don't think. Listen."

With eyes still closed, I focus my spirit on the spiritual around me. Yes, these are voices of many different languages. They are in harmony. I don't hear a chaotic sound of confusion but rather a sound of unity. Yes, they are voices that I'm hearing. Some are high pitched, and some are very low, but they all flow together.

"Very good," I hear from the Spirit of Knowledge. "The sounds are coming from the place of remembrance on your left. This is the resting place of the holy. The holy are the ones who lived a life in the natural that glorified the Father. Their spirits are forever with Him in His glory. But their bones still sing out His praises. If you look closely, you will see the trees and shrubs and grass are waving to the sound of the singing birds and voices in united harmony."

Looking through the iron fence, I see it also is swaying ever so slightly with the singing. "Yes, I see it!" I exclaim.

Then Knowledge says, "This is the part of the warfare realm the enemy has no part of. Let's continue on our walk."

We resume our walk, and I ask, "It seems odd to me that it's on the left. Why is that?"

"Direction," He says. "It's only on your left because of the direction we are walking."

"Oh, I didn't think of that," I respond. As we walk, we come to taller columns where the iron fence connects. The taller columns have a big, two-part iron gate attached to them. The gates are closed. Standing in front of the gates is a very large being with a flaming sword. I wonder....?

"Yes," Knowledge says, "a proper guard. This is an angel on assignment, placed here by the Father to guard what's holy. You notice there are no chains around its neck or holding it in place. The angels gladly do the bidding of the Father."

As we get closer, the angel tips its flaming sword towards us and holds it down as we pass. I salute from my heart with my right hand. The sword raises with a swoosh through the air. The angel resumes its position of guarding, with the sword held up in front.

This is all wonderful and amazing. This is a place in the warfare realm I didn't think existed. "Why would the Father put a place of remembrance for the holy in a realm like this?"

"Great question. Let's ponder this a bit," Knowledge says. "Understanding, what have You to say?" as He nods to defer to Her.

Understanding goes with the conversation and doesn't miss a step as we walk. "In the natural world when there is war, where are some of the warriors buried? Where are the cemeteries?"

I immediately think of Normandy and the D Day invasion. Thousands of Allied troops were killed, taking that beach. In my mind I see all the white crosses placed with precision on the graves. The mind of my spirit begins to understand. Sadly, I ask, "These are casualties of war in this realm, aren't they?"

The forms of the Spirit of Understanding and Knowledge bow their heads in confirmation to my question.

Understanding says, "Yes, gallant men and women who for some reason or another missed or didn't listen to Our guidance."

"The bones of Metak's father are here," as Knowledge points through the iron fence.

Passing by the place of remembrance, I notice the sky seems to darken on both sides of the path. I can feel the darkness. A cold chill blows over me, and my feet begin to glow from the gold soles under them. I reach to my chest to feel the sheath holding my weapons. I comment, "We have moved past the place of holy remembrance and are coming closer to the cemetery I've been in, aren't we?"

"Yes," Understanding whispers into my spirit. "Again, your perception and discernment are sharper."

The cover of the mist of Their presence thickens around us. Gazing through the mist just ahead on our right, I see we are approaching something that looks broken down. Yes, these are broken-down, stone walls. Everything is a dark gray. Beyond the broken-down places in the walls are mounds of graves, placed in circular patterns. There are no trees, no bushes, no flowers, and certainly no singing birds. I hear a high-pitched but faint scream coming from deep within that place. As we get closer, I hear snarls and shrieks. It's a dark, unpleasant place.

Coming closer yet, I hear rattling chains. Looking ahead, I see a big, ugly being with a chain wrapped twice around its neck. The chain is draped over its left shoulder and leads to a hook-shaped anchor in the ground. The big, ugly being has a rugged, dirty, rusty sword in its right hand. It holds it up in defiance to the misty cloud we are in as we pass by. Knowledge leans over to me and speaks Spirit to spirit, "Place of the dead they call it," as He points into the cemetery.

"The walls are broken down; the guard is standing, chained to the ground in front of gates that are off their hinges. What's the need for a guard when it's easily accessed?" I ponder.

Understanding says, "Counterfeit. The enemy will copy everything that is true and righteous and holy. There is no need for the walls, gates, or guards because this place can be accessed through all the open, broken-down places. But really, it's not a travel destination people want to visit. Ideals, doctrines, and gifting's are only taken there when they are stolen, and the enemy wants them hidden."

I point out, "There seem to be more graves in there than in the place of holy remembrance."

Understanding speaks Spirit to spirit, "Yes. Some rightfully so need to be there but most, like I just said, have been stolen and buried to keep them hidden."

I know She's speaking of stolen truths of the Father.

She continues, "Hidden so untruth can be propagated. Or like Us," as She nods at Knowledge, "Our godly reality stolen and replaced with a worldly aspect of Who We are. Then it is preached as truth."

She says, "We will be back here with you. The Father has more work for you and the team here."

A chill comes over my being at Her words, but it only makes me stand taller and lean into Them more.

We move quickly past the place of the dead. The gravel path winds around it and out into a vast, dark, gray, open plain. I'm glad to be past the place of the dead but know when I come back on assignment, I'll be walking in the authority and power of His Might.

The question at hand is, "What are we walking into next?"

In the far distance rolling clouds churn. We are heading towards them. The crunching of the gravel path ceases because the path has disappeared. Now only miles of sand lie in front of us. I'm thinking it would be nice to float above the sand so that we don't have to trudge through it.

Wisdom from above speaks into my spirit. "Trudging through the sand builds endurance and keeps you grounded in this realm. The times you have been lifted above the surface are when you would not have been able to stand in the violent shaking of this realm. The Father is not directing Us to lift you up to float."

The distant churning clouds are replaced by rain-drenched green trees in front of me. But as I sit, pondering in my chair on our porch, the question of where we are heading doesn't leave my spirit.

"I thank You, Papa, for this time of endurance. Please give me the strength to trudge through the sand of this place and learn the endurance You have set before me. Amen."

Check out Ed Sniadecki's other works!

OVERCOMING UNBELIEF TRILOGY

When Jesus first showed up day after day during Ed Sniadecki's morning devotional times, Ed didn't know the Father was sharing how He is preparing us, His Body, to bring restoration and redemption in these last days. Through every-day people and even saints of old, this prophetic allegory creates a profound, engaging story you won't want to put down.

The Lord revealed how people just like you and me will overcome unbelief by building His Body, joining with others, and ushering in His glory around us.

This faith-building prophetic story is for His Body, the Church, right now. Get ready to be changed.

MEET "ME" ON THE OTHER SIDE

Can a common, everyday person really move from the natural to the spiritual realm? Jesus is our example. He came from the spiritual to the natural and then He ascended back into the spiritual.

This first *CoffeeTime Chronicles* book, *meet "Me" on the other side*, captures daily accounts of one man's journey from the natural to the spiritual and back again. See how your life, like Ed's, can be transformed by an intimate walk with the Father, Jesus, and Holy Spirit.

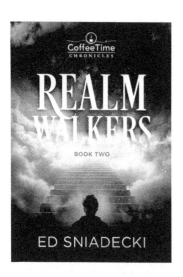

REALM WALKERS

As you read about and meditate on the God encounters in Realm Walkers, you will sense and even step into the "more" that the Father has for all His sons and daughters.

God has places, topics, and everyday experiences for all of us; it's just that some of them are not in the natural realm. Discover what the Father has for you in a realm beyond this natural realm in which we live. Become a realm walker.

Made in the USA
Columbia, SC
31 August 2024

40854755R00127